MW01235626

Don't Make Me Pull This Car Over!

A ROADMAP FOR THE WORKING MOM

BY KRISTIN ANDREE

Copyright © 2010

Cover and Interior design by Kim Barron, New Leaf Graphic Design

Printed in the U.S.A.

ISBN: 978-0-615-42123-0

No part of this publication may be reproduced or transmitted in any form or by any means, electronic or mechanical, including photocopying, recording, or any information storage and retrieval system now known or to be invented, without permission in writing from the publisher, except by a reviewer who wishes to quote brief passages in connection with a review written for inclusion in a magazine, newspaper, online publication or broadcast.

All rights reserved.

For my girls ...
Bailey, Mia, and Kennedy

* * * *

May you each find passion, power, and purpose
in the lives you create for yourselves.

* * * *

Mommy loves you!

Acknowledgments

This is the section where I get to thank the many people who have played such a pivotal role in my life ... and in the creation of this book. There are a ton of people ... and I'm sure I'll manage to forget someone, but please know that each and every one of the people I have had the pleasure (or displeasure!) of knowing throughout my life has affected me, influenced me, and helped shape me into the person I am today. So, for ALL of those experiences, I say ... "Thank you!"

Let me start with the people I have known the longest, and who have taught me more (and have put up with more!) than anyone I know. Mom, Dad, and Allen ... I love you more than you know, and your guidance, counsel, wisdom, and shoulders to cry on all these years have been invaluable. I feel so blessed to have such strong relationships with each of you. I could not have picked a better family if I tried! And to my Nana ... there isn't a day that goes by that I don't think of and miss you ... thank you for continuing to watch over me.

And since the whole premise of this book is motherhood, I must go on record to say that I could not imagine my life without my beautiful (inside and out), intelligent, crazy, fun, spirited, and amazing daughters. Bailey, Mia, and Kennedy ... I love you more than you will ever know (until you have children of your own, that is), and I cherish each and every second I am with you. You girls make me a better person, continually teach me new things about the world and about myself, and are the bright spot in each day. Of course, you lovely ladies would not have been possible had I not found my love. Shaun—what can I say?—YOU amaze me! Your strength, your wisdom, your love, and your challenging me to strive for more and to be the best me I can be are what keeps me moving forward. Through sickness and health, in plenty and in want, and through my saneness AND my absolute meltdowns (although I don't remember that one being part of our wedding vows!), you have remained unwavering in your love and dedication. I could not imagine my life without you – you are my lobster!

To my extended family: Ashton, Andrew, Sandra, Richard, Brandon, Brent, Donald, Jackie, Stacie, Donald, Regina, Deyka x 2, T.A.D., Taylor, Kendall, Pat, Andy, Grant, Darla, Maddi, Dane, Elaine, Jeanne, Steve, Brad, and Kevin ... thank you for the years of laughter, support, and love!

I hope that each of YOU will continue striving to create lives of passion and fulfillment for yourselves!

And to the girls I love so much … although I have been blessed with a wealth of friends over the years, there is a handful of you guys I couldn't live without: Leanna, Michelle, Michele, Alicia, and Stephanie (aka Farris). Your love, counsel, and friendship mean the world to me. Girlfriends really are the glue that holds us all together. Love love love y'all.

Next, I'm pretty lucky in that I have had people throughout my life to mentor me, challenge me, teach me, and sometimes just make me laugh. A little more glue holding the pieces of my crazy, fulfilled life together. From childhood through present day, I hope these people know how positively their support and encouragement have impacted me personally: Debbie Ball, John Qualy, Sabine Robinson, Phil Bender, Len DiCostanzo, Kristie Googin, Sana Ahmed, Lori Verrastro, Sue Lewandowski, Joey Davenport, Amy Medbery, Mary Lundstrom, and of course … my Bunco Babes!

My dear friend and colleague Samantha Robinson (and her fabulous hubby Doug) … there is absolutely NO way I could have brought this book to fruition without your help. Your tireless efforts in reading drafts, letting me run ideas by you, and being open and honest in your feedback were invaluable! You are an amazing talent. I couldn't ask for a better business partner! We're going to have an amazing future together!

To my fabulous editor, Marggie Graves … you are a gift (I never knew I was so bad at spelling and punctuation … please don't tell my former English teacher)! And to my graphic designer, Kim Barron … you are pure genius! Your designs are incredible and really capture my message. Plus … you two ladies are both so sweet and fun to work with!

Lastly, a million thanks to Dan Paige, Linda Howard, Jessica Bram (and your wonderful workshops), Lucy Hedrick, Jane Pollak and my entire mastermind group for your amazing input and advice … I couldn't imagine bringing this book to fruition without each of you.

"In everyone's life, at some time, our inner fire goes out. It is then burst into flame by an encounter with another human being. We should all be thankful for those people who rekindle the inner spirit."

ALBERT SCHWEITZER

CONTENTS

(Don't you skip this section ... I know how busy moms try to shortcut things!)

I'M TAKING THE KEYS ... 'CAUSE YOU'RE IN NO CONDITION TO DRIVE

OK, LADIES ... IT'S TIME TO GET SERIOUS. Time to quit your whining and choose to do something about this crazy road trip you're on. You know the one ... where you drive to work ... you drive the kids to soccer ... and gymnastics ... and piano ... and karate. And most of all ... you drive yourself CRAZY with everything you have on your plates! I've heard you out there, fussing and moaning to anyone who will listen—and then going out and doing exactly the same thing the next day! Shame on you! It's time, girls. It's time once and for all—to create the life YOU want to live.

Let me ask you: Up to this point, has your life played out *exactly* as you envisioned it when you were a little girl? Do you have the perfect career and have plenty of time for family and friends? Are you accomplishing everything you set out to do? And are you doing all of this with a sense of passion and fulfillment?

While an idyllic life with a mansion and a George Clooney-look-alike spouse may not be exactly what you are looking for, the truth is, that for the majority of us, our lives as working moms don't resemble what we thought they would by this point in our lives. If you are anything like me, you've been shooting up that ladder of success for some time now; but every so often, little (or sometimes big) hiccups come along that seem to throw your life all out of kilter. And frankly those things typically come in tiny packages (equipped with a big set of lungs and a propensity for costing us A LOT of $$$)! Let's face it: while we love those precious little darlings, sometimes they wreak havoc on our otherwise normal lives. I have to tell you, I absolutely LOVE my girls. Wouldn't trade a second with them for anything in the world (except maybe the second when one of them is screaming in the middle of the grocery store—I'd trade that second for sure!). However, despite the infinite amount of love I feel for them, they did drastically change my life—and have from the minute they entered this world.

It has been a change for the better. My life is so much fuller now that I have them to share everything with. But creating a fulfilling life takes adjustments. You have to learn to mold your life to match what you want out of it. You have to work to create an ideal schedule for your time and your energies. And you have to consciously work to fashion your life into what you want it to be. As you have probably experienced, there are huge challenges that face us as working moms and that will continue to face us. The key is to know where you stand and where you want your life to go. You must know what your values are and where your priorities lie. Through this journey, I will help you uncover many ideas and shortcuts that should be of tremendous value to you in creating a full life (one that gets fuller every day)!

Maybe you have already accomplished many of the things you set out to do, yet are craving more. Perhaps you are seeking a way to better blend your career and family lives or are looking for some tips on how to juggle all of the items on your "to-do list." Or maybe you have had it up to here and need to find a way to keep those little monsters from driving you even closer to a monthlong stay in the loony bin! If any of this strikes a chord with you, this is exactly the book for you. I am assuming you have each accomplished a lot throughout the course of your life (heck, you're a mom ... you accomplish the heroic feat of getting out of bed and facing those kids every day!). And huge congratulations on all that you have *already* achieved!

In light of this ... and before we dig into all the areas we need to work on ... let's take a moment to give ourselves a pat on the back for all that we have already accomplished. I want you to list ten accomplishments, both personal and professional, that you are proud of.

....

"I definitely deserve kudos for ..."

○ _____

○ _____

○ _____

○ _____

○ _____

○ _____

○ _____

○ _____

○ _____

○ _____

....

With all of the things we busy moms have to do in our lives, we seldom stop to pat ourselves on the back. If you haven't already, celebrate the successes you've had up to this point. Take some time to give yourself a big ol' treat. I tend to prefer a trip to the spa, but a new pair of shoes or a big serving of ice cream will work in a pinch too! This is an absolute MUST ... you have to treat yourself from time to time ... to give yourself credit for the job you're doing. Just tell your husband that this absolutely fabulous book you are reading *insists* that you reward yourself with a new pair of stilettos. (If your husband is anything like my husband, he will say you have plenty of shoes ... but trust me, ladies ... most men won't say no to a pair of stilettos ... and none of them say no to ice cream!)

Throughout this journey, my vision for you is that we take all that you have accomplished and bump it up a notch (or ten notches). No matter what you have accomplished in your life, there is always something else. Something bigger to strive for. The moment you stop living for something, you die. The moment you choose to stop reaching for more—to stop growing—you will begin to shrink away. As someone whose mission it is to "coach, challenge, and empower others to lead passion-filled, powerful, and prosperous lives," I refuse to let that happen to you. Through this book, my goal is that each of you walks away with a clear plan for creating the life you want—a well-defined strategy for creating the life you've imagined. Not just a tip or two, but a fully defined, well-thought-out PLAN!

We're going to share some stories and some laughs. And most importantly, we're going to let you know that you're not alone. ALL of us have challenges … all of us have the occasional breakdown … and IT'S OK! I truly believe you CAN have it all (just not all at the same time!). Some hours need to be work-focused; others are meant for the kids. Some times are set apart for you to hang with the girls, and others for you and your spouse to "talk" up in your room (with the door locked, of course!). The key is to learn how to intertwine those moments into a passionate and purposeful life. And that is exactly what we're going to do on this journey.

This book is different from other parenting books and takes a wildly different approach from any other tips you'll glean from a magazine article. I am not Suzy Homemaker or a diva of the kitchen. I am not a MacGyver type who excels at children's art projects and science fairs. I am a mom … a hard-working, Type A mom, who puts everything I have into my career AND everything I have into my personal life. I have challenges just like the rest of you and work to juggle all the things on my to-do list each and every day. The difference is that I have developed a plan that I follow to help me get the most out of my life. A plan to *choose* the direction of my life and to actively work to create the life I want for me and for my family. This is the plan I will share with all of you lovely ladies out there!

You're not going to read about how to be the perfect mom … because, frankly, the perfect mom doesn't exist. Our goal is for you to be the best YOU … whatever that may look like!

My journey did not come without challenges. And, as we embark on this journey together, let me give you a little background about me and provide insight into why I am so passionate about helping you create a better life for yourself, one where you feel you are on a path to living the life you crave.

Just over seven years ago, I had one child, was miserable in my career, hated where I lived, and had just separated from my husband of seven years (you know what they say about that seven-year itch … well, I took it to extremes). To the casual observer, I had, up to that point, been leading a great life … I had a great job (which I was good at) and a beautiful daughter, and was on an upward trajectory—or so it appeared. I seemed to have it all together, and it looked like I knew exactly what I wanted. But that was all a façade. I wasn't really passionate about my job. To me, it was just a job … not a calling. And I had no idea what I really wanted to do with my life. To top it off, I was making ALL of the classic mommy mistakes (late pickups, forgetting activities, not spending quality time with my child). Plus, I had been putting absolutely NO time into working on my relationship with my spouse! On most days, I was satisfied with just keeping my head above water! It was all I could do to keep from drowning in my endless, yet meaningless, list of to-dos. It sucked!

Fast-forward to today, when I have three fabulous children (loud, a little crazy, but still fabulous!) and a thriving business (which I absolutely love). I have relocated to a new city (a Southern girl living in the Northeast … watch out, world!), and have a solid marriage (go figure … to the same husband I separated from years ago).

So, how did I get from point A to point B? From a life devoid of joy and fulfillment to the exciting yet busy life I lead today? To start, I became extremely clear on what I wanted out of my life and then I set out on a journey to get there (with the help, of course, of my family and a wealth of others). What I hope to share in this book is a road map for YOU to create the passionate, fulfilled life that YOU desire—whether you are already on your way to that life or are currently as unfulfilled and discontent as I was. It took some real work on my part, and it will take some real work on yours. But I have faith you can pull it off—that you can create as full a life as you can vividly imagine.

But don't think it's gonna be a cakewalk! I did not design this book simply to be a quick read, but rather a journey for you to travel through. It is filled with exercises for you to complete and checklists at the end of each chapter. You're all working moms, and I know how we Type A personalities can't wait to check something off our list—so I thought I'd give you an opportunity to do just that each and every chapter!

So, let's get crackin' …

····· *Chapter 1* ·····

THERE'S NO OWNER'S MANUAL FOR LIFE

*"Think of yourself as on the threshold of
unparalleled success. A whole, clear, glorious life
lies before you. Achieve! Achieve!"*

— ANDREW CARNEGIE

ADMIT IT … YOU'RE A LITTLE SCREWY IN THE HEAD.
Just yell it out—"I must be nuts!" Go ahead and do it—you'll feel a
definite sense of relief. I mean, who else would sign up for a job that pays
only in hugs (and last time I checked, I couldn't pay for those Manolos
with 750 hugs!), and on top of that will COST us several hundred
thousand dollars! Who else would put their lives almost completely on
hold so that their family has exactly what they need and want?

The answer is simple: **The Working Mom!**

Rarely has one group of people given so much and expected (or
should I say tolerated?) so little in return. I'm not here to ask you to
stop giving … or to stop loving. Instead, I am here to create a shift in
your thinking and in the way you approach "working motherhood."
It's interesting how you never hear anyone say someone is a "working
father." That is simply because, as women, we are expected to do it all.
And, unfortunately, many women do that at the expense of their own
happiness. We can only give of ourselves when we are in a good place.
And I want to challenge each of you to find that place. To create the life
YOU want—to change the way you are going through life, so that you can

be a better mom, a better spouse, and a better YOU!

The first step in creating this life is to get your head on straight. You must start this journey with both a clear head and a clean slate. One of the reasons many people fail when they set out to make a change is that they simply let negative thoughts and "I can'ts" get in the way of the changes they are trying to make. You must be clear that you and you alone CHOOSE how you react to your situation and how you will listen to and implement guidance from this book and from those around you. You have to be ready for a change … you have to want it … and you have to *make* it happen. I am of the belief that things don't happen to you! You choose the course of your life by the way you react to the things going on around you. And by what you choose to focus on.

In his book *The Strangest Secret,* Earl Nightingale pointed out how our thoughts and actions shape our lives when he likened our minds to the earth. He stated that, like the earth, our minds do not care what we plant in them. He pointed out that the earth will return whatever is planted—be it a poisonous plant or a nutritious crop. Our minds, like the earth, return what we plant. If we continually feed it negative thoughts of why we cannot accomplish something, that is exactly what it will return. Have you ever seen this play out with someone you know? Where she did nothing but feed her mind with negative thoughts? My guess is that the person you are envisioning is not a success in her career or life. Am I right?

If you are to be a success in life and lead the life you truly desire, it is imperative that you don't let negative thoughts run your day. The mind and the attitude work like anything else: garbage in … garbage out! So, as we travel this journey together, let's keep the garbage the heck away from us! Throughout this process, focus on what you want and envision that you are already there!

A few years ago, I worked with a woman who was the classic example of someone *choosing* to focus only on the negatives and to feed her mind with poison. In doing so, she wasted time on things that were simply not important in the grand scheme of her life. She spent most of her workday overreacting to the things that "happened" to her and wasting precious time and energy existing in a negative mental state.

She was an intelligent girl with a lot of gifts to give, but she didn't see it. And she refused to actually use the talents she had. She spent most of her time complaining about all that she had to do (and quite frankly, she really did very little work compared with the rest of our new associates), and she spent the remainder of her workday telling us why anything we suggested that might help her "would never work." She said that between taking the kids to day care, dealing with sick kiddos, and taking the car in for service, she couldn't get everything done. Really? Do any of you NOT have to deal with these things? As working moms, those are all part of our (very long) job description. We ALL have child-care issues. ALL of our cars break down from time to time. It's a part of life that we ALL must learn to manage.

I can tell you exactly why this woman wasn't a success in our business. And it had nothing to do with all the things that "happened" to her. If she spent even half the time she spent bitchin' about her circumstances on something productive ... like, I don't know, *doing some actual work* ... she would have been great. She was feeding her mind full of nothing but negative thoughts ... of garbage. Every day she was making a conscious choice to remain in the same place. Every day she was choosing not to grow. And every day she was choosing not to move her life in the direction of her dreams.

I hated to see her fail. I hate to see anyone fail. But there is one thing you have to realize when challenging people to grow, and that is: they have to want to change! They have to be ready and willing to grow. My questions for you then are: Do you want to grow? Are you ready to take control of your life? To take the necessary steps to create the life you want and work toward creating this new fabulous life of yours?

○ Yes   ○ No

If you cannot answer unequivocally yes to this question, I want you to stop for a minute and think about where you are in your life. Have you gotten everything out of life that you want? If so, congratulations, and further congratulations on continuing to invest in your growth by reading this book to help you succeed even more.

If not, I need you to make a commitment to change. Right now, I want you to commit to giving your absolute best to this journey. I'm not asking for your firstborn here (although some of you might be willing to give them up!). I am asking only for your commitment to *work* at becoming the best YOU! In return, I commit to do my best to guide you every step of the way. I ask that you embark on this journey with an open mind and with a pledge of working to create the life you desire ... the one you were meant to lead.

The choice people make not to grow, to remain exactly where they are, is extremely frustrating for me ... as a leader, as a friend, and as a working mom. The frustration I feel from seeing people not living the life they desire, like the former associate I described above, is what drove me to write this book. I plan to keep challenging and motivating others, but I want to give other women the tools to get out of *their* slumps and begin to create the extraordinary lives they desire.

Again, this journey will not be without difficulty and will take a lot of work. It will require some changes. And some of these changes may be drastic, but know that they are necessary. I promise you ... the changes you will make in your life and the impact they will have on your confidence, your energy, your career, AND your family will far outweigh any challenges you may encounter.

As we begin our journey, it is necessary to get a sense of what you stand for and a sense of what you really want out of life. To do this, we must first get clear on what it is you value. What are the *core values* that shape your decision making? Frequently we hear companies touting their values via a commercial or at a company meeting. You may hear something like "We pride ourselves on our integrity and our commitment to excellence." But what is it YOU value as an *individual*? Have you taken the time to dive in and really explore this? In my coaching work with professionals, I have found that most seasoned execs have typically done some sort of exercise (usually at a leadership retreat somewhere) where they outlined their personal values. But most people, especially young professionals, newer to the workforce, have never taken time to determine what they value above all else. This is very disheartening, as values are what drive us (or at least what *should* drive us) in our decision-making process.

Let's start by defining the word "value." Webster's defines a value as "something (as a principle or quality) intrinsically valuable or desirable."

That sounds pretty good. But let's go a bit deeper. One definition that has always resonated with me is that a value is "something you hold so dear that you are willing to stand up for it … even in the face of adversity." That says something. It says that once you have defined your values, you should hold each and every action and each and every decision up to them to determine if what you are doing or are about to do is in alignment with your values. If you do so, you can move forward with confidence that you are on the right path. If, however, your actions aren't in alignment with your values, you are probably moving ahead with something you will feel uncomfortable with and may later regret. Knowing your values shapes the decisions you make every day and makes it easy to know which path to take with sometimes-difficult decisions.

For me, the following are the things I hold dear:
- Integrity
- Passion
- Empowerment
- Personal Growth

Each time I am presented with a decision or an opportunity, I hold it up to my values to check for alignment. Doing this hasn't guided me wrong yet. (I get in trouble only when I forget to do a values check before jumping into something!) There have been times throughout my career when people have urged me to do something that I didn't feel was quite right (we've all been faced with these types of things, right?). When you can look them in the eye and tell them that what they are asking of you flies in the face of your values, what can they do? Tell you that you don't have values? Or that your values are wrong? Heck, no! No one would do that. They may still try to persuade you to move forward with whatever it is they are pushing, but that is their business. If you stand your ground and stick to your values, you can't be wrong. Remember the definition of a value … "something you hold so dear that you are willing to stand up for it … *even in the face of adversity*." That last part is key.

It's easy to tout our values when the stakes are low or the decision to be made is an easy one. It's not quite as easy when our relationships or our jobs are on the line. And this is when we need our values the most.

This is when they are critical. I want you to hear me on this point ... and know that this is nonnegotiable: *If someone wants you to do something that flies in the face of your values, you don't need that person!* If a relationship is threatened because you won't compromise on a values-based decision, drop that relationship. If your employer asks you to compromise your value system, find another employer. There are a plethora of people out there to love, challenge, and support you without making you compromise your values. And there are a ton of companies out there in which you will never be asked to go against your values. You've just got to find 'em.

Let's spend some time now defining YOUR values so that you will have a better understanding of what you need to be holding up when you make all the decisions you're bound to face. Start by looking at the list below and circling all of the values that apply to you (feel free to add any of your own to the list). If you have previously defined your values, use this as an opportunity to ensure that they still ring true.

Achievement	Integrity	Quality
Adventure	Intellectual	Recognition
Challenge	Involvement	Religion
Charity	Knowledge	Reputation
Close Relationships	Leadership	Responsibility
Commitment	Learning	Security
Community	Love	Self-Respect
Competence	Loyalty	Serenity
Empathy	Merit	Spirituality
Empowerment	Passion	Stability
Friendships	Personal Development	Status
Fun	Personal Growth	Truth
Growth	Personal Responsibility	Variety
Harmony	Pleasure	Wisdom
Helping Others	Power	_____
Honesty	Prestige	_____
Independence	Public Service	_____
Influence	Purity	_____

Since we can't walk around touting twenty-eight values (it'd take us FOREVER to make a decision if we had to hold something up to every one of them), we need to start narrowing down our list a bit. I want you to look at the values you circled and begin to narrow your list down to ten. Write those values in the box below.

Top Ten Values

1 _____ 2 _____

3 _____ 4 _____

5 _____ 6 _____

7 _____ 8 _____

9 _____ 10 _____

Now, I want you to narrow it down even further … to the ones that will form the foundation of your decisions and how you behave every day. Write the **Top Five Values** that resonate with you in the box on the following page. When you get to this stage, it sometimes becomes difficult to narrow it down further. You feel like they all represent you. And they do. But you need to pick the ones that *really* capture you. Frequently, you may have identified two values that are very similar (such as Integrity and Honesty). If this is the case, consider picking one of them to move forward on your list.

Top Five Values

1. ....

2. ....

3. ....

4. ....

5. ....

Here is the final purging … narrow your list down just a smidge more. I want you to choose three (four, tops) values, which will be your **CORE VALUES**—the ones you hold so dear you will stand up for them, even if you are faced with adversity. Write them in the boxes below.

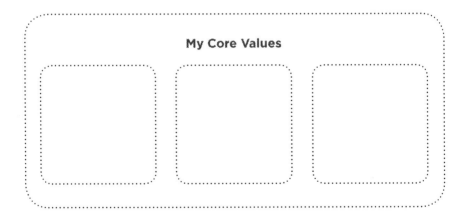

My Core Values

Now that you have defined your Core Values and have a sense of what you stand for, we need to take the next step on our journey.

If you are going to work on creating the life you desire, you must start by defining what that means to you. It means different things to different people. For some, it may have a financial component. For others, it means having more time to spend with their loved ones. What does it mean to YOU? Don't try to compare yourself with the media "supermom" or with the celeb moms you see on TV. You know the ones, looking gorgeous while they balance their careers with a seemingly happy and harmonious home life. Here's the real scoop: these people have multiple nannies, a driver, a personal trainer, a chef … and a housekeeper! For most moms, that just isn't realistic. Instead, think of the things that will make YOU happy (if it's a nanny and a chef, so be it—just make sure it's what YOU truly want … and that you're not just putting it on the list because your friend Susie has a personal chef). What is it that will make YOU feel that you are leading a purposeful, fulfilled life? Begin by completing the following statement:

"When I think of the life I want to lead, this is what I have in mind..."

• _____

• _____

• _____

• _____

• _____

Now that you have begun to define what your ideal life means to you, let's make sure that you have broken it down to what you *really* want. Look at each of the points above and ask yourself to break them down even further. For example, if you said part of "having it all" means having a $1 million salary, why is that? What do you want that salary to do for you? If you wrote down that you wanted more freedom, ask yourself: freedom to do what? The clearer and more specific you can be, the easier it will be for you to visualize what you are striving for. If you define a full life by your ability to "keep up with the Joneses," then, quite frankly, you're an idiot! And suffice it to say that you will never achieve true happiness. Only when you go after and attain those things that matter to *you* will you be fulfilled.

Finally, as we continue working on the areas of your life (personal and professional) that will move you in the direction of leading a fulfilled life, it is imperative that you find someone to help you along your journey. This trip will not be without difficulty and will require action on your part (come on, ladies … you've been looking for a little action, right?). Your experience will be far more beneficial and you will have a much greater likelihood of following through if you have someone else holding you accountable for implementing the recommendations in this book. I highly recommend your spouse (if he/she is a willing participant). If not, ask a girlfriend who needs to get a little more action in her own life to read the book with you. You can keep each other in check. Whoever you choose as your accountability partner needs to care about you. She needs to have your best interest at heart and genuinely want to help you work to improve your life (just as you have to genuinely want to improve yourself). Above all, your partner must be able to speak up and tell you what you need to hear, not just what you want to hear. She has to be OK with getting in your face and telling you like it is. That friend who actually tells you when the dress makes you look fat … that's *exactly* who you're looking for here!

Tackle one chapter at a time—and make sure you fully embrace and implement the ideas from that chapter. Discuss the ideas from each chapter with your accountability partner to clue her in on what you are working on—so your partner can make sure you are sticking to your plan.

I want you to lead better lives and to reach new heights. To do so, I am going to make it easier for you to follow through with the ideas you learn. As you have seen in this initial chapter, the book contains exercises to help you clarify the items you are working on. And here is the first of many checklists you will find along your journey. Checklists are one of the best ways to ensure that things get done. Ask your accountability partner to work with you to ensure that you are implementing the ideas contained in each chapter into your daily life … both at work and at home. Your partner's reward … a happier, more fulfilled (and more fun to be around) you! Of course, you could also bribe your partner with a cosmo or mojito (which, truth be told, might help her be a bit more candid and honest in her feedback!).

Here's to checking things off our list, ladies …

CHECKLIST

O Commit to the journey (and I mean commit … just like in poker, you've got to be "all in"). To signify your commitment to this whole process, I want you to sign on the dotted line.

"I, _____, commit to giving my absolute best on this journey toward a more fulfilled life. I promise to complete all the exercises and to work with (and listen to) my accountability partner (even when I totally don't want to hear it!).
I will allow myself to make mistakes and will forgive myself when I do! If I get off-track, I'll forgive myself … and then I'll get back on the horse and try again.
Here we go … it's gonna be a fun ride!"

Signed,

_____

O Define your values (and tell your accountability partner, your spouse, and everyone else all about them!).

My CORE VALUES are:

• _____

• _____

• _____

(continued ..)

CHECKLIST (continued)

O Define the life you desire (and don't forget to break it all the way down).

To me, "the life I want to lead" entails:

- _____

- _____

- _____

- _____

- _____

O Find an accountability partner to share what you have learned and to make sure you are actually incorporating the ideas from this book into your life.

My accountability partner is:_____

····· *Chapter 2* ·····

CHECK OUT THOSE STANDARD FEATURES

"Some men throw their gifts away on a life of mediocrity, great men throw everything they have into their gifts and achieve a life of success."

— GREG WERNER

HAVE YOU EVER HEARD IT SAID THAT SOMEONE WAS "BORN TO" DO SOMETHING? I am sure that at some point in our lives each of us has either heard something of the sort or even said it about someone we know. "He was born to perform" or "She is a natural when it comes to tennis." Each of us is born with innate gifts that, if uncovered and cultivated, can lead us to a life of extraordinary accomplishments.

Now, if we were only born with a list of those unique gifts (or even a clue as to what they may be) … or a list of the strengths we should work on cultivating. It would sure as heck make things a lot easier on us. Or at least point us in the right direction. But we aren't born with such a list. Not even close. We come into this world without a clue as to what our innate strengths are. Not even the new parents we have just graced with our presence have a clue as to what it is we are destined to do (although if your mother is anything like mine, I'm sure she gave you a few suggestions!).

Since there is no road map, we have to create one for ourselves. And that is exactly what we are going to spend some time on here. If we are ever to put our God-given gifts to good use, we must first discover what they are! I am of the belief that each and every one of us is born with special gifts or strengths, something innate, that, if cultivated, will lead us toward great lives of purpose. I believe that *everyone* was created for a reason and that there is something good in each of us. Our job is to find out what that is and work our darndest to use our strengths to contribute to the world—in whatever way fuels our passions (we'll talk more about our passions in the next chapter). No one is exempt from this. The people you encounter who are walking around miserable and hating their lives haven't discovered this very powerful fact. They are miserable because they are neglecting the very things that are inherent in their makeup.

Are you one of those people? Are you walking around miserable—feeling like you are wasting your God-given talent? If so, you have to change … and change NOW.

Throughout our lives, there are numerous ways people try to uncover our strengths, to unlock the mystery of what we are supposed to be doing with our lives. We have all seen a number of tests that are "supposed to" tell us what we should be when we grow up. They take into account all of our personality traits, mix them together with the subjects we seem to excel at in school, feed that data into their database of occupations, and magically tell us what we are destined to do with our lives! Now, I am not an expert in these types of tests, by any means. However, what I can tell you is that most of the tests I have seen are a load of crap. They come out telling someone who is good at science that she should be a scientist! Well, thanks for the infinite words of wisdom, Nostradamus! I could have figured that one out for myself.

I am challenging each of you to go deeper than that. Not to look at what occupation you should work in per se, but rather to explore what your unique strengths are, so that you can apply them to whatever it is you set out to do.

You see, to truly be happy with what you are doing with your life, you need to be doing something you are good at. It's only common sense, right? Do something you suck at … people see that you suck at it … you feel miserable. It is inevitable. No one who is knowingly incompetent at something can really find satisfaction doing that something day in and day out to earn a living. Now, if you don't realize you are incompetent, that's a whole different ballgame. (I'm not naming any names here … just sayin'!). To lead a full life, where you feel you have it all, there are two things you MUST incorporate into your career: First, you must work within an area of strength for yourself. Second, you must do something you are passionate about. And these are not mutually exclusive—you must have them BOTH. And since those career tests don't really seem to do the trick, what do you do to uncover your true strengths and your passions?

In this chapter, we are going to look into uncovering your innate gifts or strengths. Then, in the next chapter, we'll layer in the next piece … uncovering and following the things you are passionate about.

Too often I see companies and managers speak of people's "strengths AND weaknesses." They identify what people are good at and then take it a step further and identify areas where they are not so good and label them "weaknesses." I mean, come on—who likes to be told she is "weak" at something? The very connotation is depressing. I hear managers say they need to uncover their employees' weaknesses so that they can "work on them" and "turn them into strengths." Are you flippin' kidding me? This has always been counterintuitive to me. I operate with a preference of working to cultivate people's gifts as opposed to spending the bulk of time on their perceived "weaknesses."

If we spend most of our time working on our weaknesses, we end up with really strong weaknesses! But they are still that … weaknesses! They will never be strengths for us, because they are not what we *naturally* excel at. Bernard Haldane, a pioneer in positive psychology, in the 1950s, years ahead of his time, suggested that we focus on people's positive traits as opposed to focusing on negative aspects. He put it so well: "If you want to get the best out of a man, you must look for the best that is in him." And that is precisely what we are going to do here—discover the best that is in you! When you meet new people and interact with them, you can try to see the good, or you can see the bad. CHOOSE to see the best in people. And when you find the best that is in people, make it your charge to cultivate that strength. To make it even better, even stronger.

Sure, our strengths may change a bit over time as we encounter different life experiences, but, to an extent, we are born with most of them … and it is our responsibility to cultivate them. I have worked throughout my own life to discover the strengths I possess. Although my younger brother would likely still contend that I am not good at anything (jealousy, I am sure!), I think I have finally settled on a few key areas where I consistently tend to excel. (I was lucky enough to find one great assessment some years back, which helped me further solidify my strengths … highly recommend it … see my recommended reading list at the back of the book for that one!) I have discovered that two areas of strength for me are *communication* and *developing people*.

As you can see, these strengths don't outline the occupations I should work in or any particular jobs for which I should apply. They simply and succinctly outline the areas where I tend to excel. And by knowing these, I have been able to incorporate them into my career and into my life.

At the time I worked to define my strengths, some nine years ago, I was in a strictly sales job. Now I know what you're thinking here: "Kristin, how could you not have been totally and completely psyched about your career? After all, you were selling *insurance*!" That's everyone's dream job, right? For the most part, I did like my job (truth be told … it is an excellent profession and a tremendous way to help people) and was doing well at it, but it wasn't fulfilling me. Sure, I was having a significant impact on the lives of my clients, but I was craving something more.

Once I took a closer look at the things I was uniquely qualified to do and the things I genuinely loved to do, I was able to begin to incorporate them into my career. I began to recruit and mentor new associates (fulfilling my desire to develop others) and later accepted a position with our company's corporate office that provided me an opportunity to do a TON of speaking engagements (while this may seem pretty scary to most, for someone with the gift of gab … or communication … as a key strength, I was in my element). And, most recently with writing this book and continuing with speaking engagements, I am striving to develop people on a much larger stage.

It doesn't matter what your particular strengths are. What matters is that you recognize them and work to put them to good use. It's like the saying "Use your powers for good." When you become more in touch with your strengths, and work to incorporate them into what you are doing career-wise, you'll be a happy camper. When your job leads you into areas where you are not continually working in your strengths, you will likely be miserable! Work to consciously create these opportunities for yourself (and for your sanity). Just think: if we all worked in areas where we excelled, look how productive and powerful we would be. Many companies today are working to become more aware of the job satisfaction of their employees and will work with you to create opportunities for you to shine (we'll address the companies that don't in Chapter 4).

As perfect a world as it would be if we ALL loved 100 percent of our work day in and day out, that isn't always possible. The 80/20 rule definitely applies here. While you should strive to LOVE at least 80 percent of your job, there will likely always be 20 percent that is just a necessary evil. (For me, this falls into the categories of paperwork and bookkeeping; for others, paperwork may be your passion!) But, hey, if we ALL get to a solid 80 percent, we're doing pretty darn good.

So, what are YOUR strengths? What are the things you excel at? Or, looking at it a different way, what drives you? Sometimes a strength can be the way in which we are motivated to succeed—as with someone striving for recognition or desiring to reach a certain position or possess a certain degree of power. Here are a few choices to stimulate your thinking. Circle those that resonate with you. If other things pop into your head, jot them down too. The key is to uncover three or four strengths that we will work to ensure play an active role in your career and in your life.

Public Speaking	Writing	Developing Others
Performing	Analytical Skills	Connecting with People
Quest for Knowledge	Intuition	Listening
Determination	Communication	Planning/Organization
Artistic	Creativity	Teaching
Leadership	Relationships	Collaboration
Service	Having an Impact	Enthusiasm
_____	_____	_____
_____	_____	_____

Now, give this list to someone or even a couple of people who know you well (perhaps your accountability partner) and see what they come up with. This will give you some valuable insight into what others perceive to be your strengths.

Which of the areas that you or your partners outlined above do you feel are your Top Three? The ones you absolutely connect with on every level? The ones that, if incorporated into your career and into your personal life, would help you achieve a greater level of satisfaction in your job and your life?

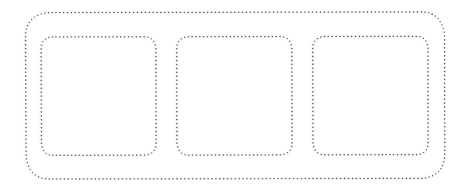

Now that we have identified these, let's take it a step further. Look at the three areas you just identified. Ask yourself, "Does area No. 1 have a prominent place in my career? Does No. 2? What about No. 3?"

If you can HONESTLY answer "yes" to these questions, you have done a good job thus far of incorporating your talents into your current career—whether knowingly or unwittingly. You may still have some degree of dissatisfaction with your career for other reasons (which we will cover in the following chapters), but for the most part you are making sure you are able to utilize your gifts.

If you answered "no," you've got bigger problems. If you haven't yet had the opportunity to utilize your innate strengths, I see two HUGE problems:

Problem No. 1: You are WAY underperforming.
You have to be—you aren't firing on all cylinders. In fact, you're not even lighting up the cylinders that are any good! To put it in more simplistic

and easier to visualize terms—you've got a swimsuit model body and are walking around wearing a muumuu. You've heard the adage "If you've got it, flaunt it." Same goes for your career—if you've got a particular strength, and that strength excites you, show it off to the world. Use it, and incorporate it into your career. If not, it's a slap in the face to those of us who would love to but don't possess your particular talent. (For example, I would LOVE to be able to sing and perform … but have absolutely NO artistic ability in that arena. As my husband puts it, my voice "is like nothing you've ever heard!")

Read back over the quote at the beginning of the chapter. Are YOU throwing your gifts away on a life of mediocrity? Or can you do better? WILL YOU do better?

Problem No. 2: You have GOT TO be miserable with what you are doing.

We've heard it before—"life's too short." And it sure as hell is too short to be wasting it doing a half-ass job in a career where we aren't able to be the best we can be and aren't putting our God-given talents to work. I believe we were put on this earth for a reason—to make it a better place for those who come after us, and to have fun doing it! You can't do that when your "career half" isn't having any fun!

So, how do we put our strengths to work (or how do we work them at capacity)? It starts by having an awareness of your natural talents and gifts. We have done that here. Next, you need to continually look for opportunities to put your strengths to good use—whether in your career or outside. If you excel at developing people, offer to mentor an up-and-comer in your industry. If you excel at writing, ask to do an article for your company newsletter. If you are a skilled orator, volunteer to give a keynote address at your next company meeting or volunteer to present at career day at your child's school.

To start, *how* you incorporate your strengths is less important than the fact that you ARE incorporating them. Once you experience the satisfaction you gain from working in your strengths, you will naturally begin to seek out more opportunities to do so.

At that point, you can strategically choose the things that will help to advance your career and give you more responsibility or create potential new ventures for you (wherever your gifts may lead you). As the quote at the beginning of the chapter proclaimed—throw everything you have into your gifts and you will achieve a life of success.

So, what now? What you gonna put on that checklist of yours for this chapter? This one I am going to leave *entirely* up to you. For this chapter's checklist, I want YOU to list three to five things you will do that will allow you to utilize your unique gifts—either in your career or in your personal life. Remember to put a target completion date to help hold you to it. Here we go …

CHECKLIST

WHAT?	BY WHEN?
1	
2	
3	
4	
5	

····· Chapter 3 ·····

THE JOURNEY IS THE DESTINATION

"There is no passion to be found playing small – in settling for a life that is less than the one you are capable of living."

— NELSON MANDELA

NOW THAT YOU HAVE DEFINED WHAT "LIVING THE LIFE YOU DESIRE" MEANS TO YOU, and have determined the areas in which you possess natural strengths, let's take a few more steps and figure out WHO you really are. For many of the people I have come across, their true selves have seemed to fade away over the years. As busy working moms, we sometimes have a tendency to blend into the background. To take a back seat to what our children do. I swear to you … I don't know the actual names of half of the moms at my kids' school … they are known only as "Hannah's mom" or "Parker's mom." How pathetic is that? Is that really what we wanted to be?

How many of you can remember what you first wanted to be when you grew up (and I bet it wasn't "Hunter's mommy"!)? Or what your interests were while you were in high school? For me, I wanted to open my own clothing store. OK, OK, there was that brief stint in fifth grade when two friends and I wanted to be truck drivers, but that quickly passed. We had our lives all planned out. We had picked out our very own "big rig"—pink, of course—and planned to tour the country together. Apparently we were way ahead of our time on the concept of "job sharing," but the fact that we would have to split our income three ways must have escaped us! But, I digress …

Since I can remember, I have always had a love for fashion. My Nana had always worked in retail, and I thought it was the coolest thing in the world. I loved to go into the store where she worked and loved to check out all the cool new trends and try on all the clothes (even though they were WAY too big for me … remember those days, ladies, when the clothes we tried on were actually too BIG for us! Ah, the joy of youth!). So when did that passion for fashion fade? When did I move away from my dream of working in the fashion industry? Honestly, I have absolutely no idea. Like most of us, the dream I had as a child just seemed to fade away. If I think hard, I am sure I can come up with a time when someone told me that it wasn't practical to work in the fashion industry or that it was too hard.

I remember a brief stint in high school when I thought it would be cool to be a doctor. And then a neighbor of ours, an orthopedic surgeon, said to me: "If I had it to do all over again, I don't know if I would have done it." He went on to explain that the schooling was just way too intense. And in that brief encounter, there went the thought of being a surgeon! The problem wasn't with what he said to me; it was the fact that I listened! As children and teens, we were very impressionable, just as our children are today. And the things that were said to us as children likely had a lasting impact on our lives.

I am reminded of a quote that is frequently said in my former firm: "Do you have any idea the impact of what you say and do has on those around you?" I want you to think about that quote. Think of the impact people have had on your life. Think of the impact you are having on others. Have you, throughout your life, allowed others to steer you away from your passions? Have you listened to the naysayers when you wanted to live out your passion? Did your mom tell you that "it is too hard to make it as an actress"? Or perhaps your dad told you that you should do something practical, like get an MBA.

The point is this … throughout our lives, starting as small children, we have a number of ideas of what we want to be when we grow up. And I'd be willing to bet that the ideas you were most excited about as a child were the very ones where someone told you that the job was too hard or that it wasn't practical or even that that particular career didn't pay well. What a horrible thing to say to a child … what a horrible thing to say to anyone. But the real problem, again, is not what was said; it was the fact that we listened. As youngsters, we were not equipped with the tools and the strength to stick up for our passions. That ends NOW. From this point forward, I want you to work to continually "live with passion" (to quote Tony Robbins). In this chapter, we will discover how.

After many years in the workforce, I know one thing for sure. And that is, if you love what you do … truly love and enjoy your chosen profession … it won't seem like work at all. Sure, there will be good days and bad days; but if the work you do fulfills you, everything else just seems to fall into place.

As I mentioned, I have made a couple of career changes as I worked my way up in the corporate world. Each time I have had a renewed energy for what I was doing. At first, I thought the excitement came from the newness of the position. But in retrospect, what was bringing me excitement and fulfillment was that I was slowly moving toward what I wanted to do with my life and toward positions that increasingly used my God-given strengths and talents. I was uncovering my passion … my passion for empowering others! Sure, I still love fashion, but now I get to enjoy fashions as a *consumer* (which, to toot my own horn a bit, I am really good at!).

With this chapter we will do three things. First, I want to help you uncover *your* true passions. Second, I want to help you chart a course that allows you to follow those passions. And finally, I want to help you implement some strategies to ensure you are living out your passions in your life.

Uncovering Your Passions

So, what are the things that you are truly passionate about? The things that, if you were doing them continually as a part of your daily grind, would excite and energize you? Have you ever really thought about it? Over the years, most of us have just sort of sunk into a bit of a rut. It isn't really that we *dislike* what we are doing every day … we just like it less than we used to. You know, some of the "new car smell" has just kind of worn off. And the things that used to excite us about our careers seem to have faded a bit. Does this describe anyone you know? Does it describe you?

Many of the women I have worked with over the years (and the men, for that matter) complain of exactly that. They go to their jobs and their careers every day, complaining every step of the way. They yell at the people in traffic in the morning, fuss at the long lines at the drive-through for lunch, and spend an hour once they get home complaining how hectic and awful their day was! What a pitiful way to waste away your life.

I want you to think about your career. Really think about it. And let me ask you: Does your career fulfill you? Or is it just a means to a paycheck? Do you get excited about going to work? About the impact you make during the course of the day? Or do you watch the clock tick by and wait until it's time for you to get the heck outta Dodge, realizing that you are just going through the motions and having little to no impact on anything that is at all important to you? You need to be (or to quickly become) one of those people who find excitement and passion in their work. We are put on this earth to make an impact ... to leave this world better than we found it. And the beauty of it is that we have all been given gifts and strengths that will allow us to do just that.

So, how do we determine what we are passionate about? And how can we incorporate that into our career and our lives? Let's start with a bit of introspection. I want you to close your eyes for a minute and think about the answers to the following questions:

- What do you do when you have a couple of hours to yourself? (Aside from napping ... I have yet to find a career that centers on being able to sleep all day ... but if you know of one, I'm all ears!)
- What do you think about when you are daydreaming? (Besides Brad Pitt ... again, no career centering on watching hot guys parade by ... as nice as that would be!)
- What section do you gravitate toward in the bookstore?

I find that the answers to these simple questions often provide clues to what passions lie within us. For years, I have been drawn toward self-help and motivational books. Every time we walk into Borders, my husband, Shaun, makes a beeline for the music and photography sections and I wander off to the self-help shelves. No wonder he has found so much excitement in his career ... he is doing exactly the things he is passionate about. And no wonder I have, over the years, molded my career to allow me to have more of an impact on people, and on helping them create stronger, more powerful, and passionate lives for themselves. It is what gives me my energy … my juice! I get more excited seeing one of my associates or clients hit her goals than I do when I hit my own. I truly love to see people improve their lives by succeeding at the things they set out to do. And the coolest thing is that as a byproduct of their successes, I am achieving my goals as well.

The key is in the passion. When you are truly passionate about what you are doing, it doesn't seem like work. Not only will your work fly by, but it will also begin to seamlessly mesh with your life. It won't feel as if it is a daily grind, but rather will be your *chosen* profession, one that you deliberately and purposefully chose—to not only make your life better, but also to enrich the lives of others. I like this quote by H. Jackson Brown Jr.: "Find a job you like and you add five days to every week."

What are you passionate about? What things, if you could mold them into your career and your life, would make you a more fulfilled person? Maybe you are passionate about empowering others. Perhaps you are passionate about the environment or about making your community more beautiful or safer. Are you passionate about a particular product or company? Or do you get excitement working in a particular industry (such as aeronautics or medicine)? Whatever it is, I want you to write it here.

I am truly passionate about:

_____

_____

_____

_____

_____

Read over what you have just written here. Is this truly what you are passionate about, or have you just written what you think you should have written based on the job you have or the industry in which you work? In order to get true fulfillment from what you do, you have to find excitement and passion in it. Enough of this going through the motions crap! If you want to lead a life you absolutely love, with every inch of your being, you have to cultivate fulfillment in all areas of your life. It's not enough to just earn a paycheck. If you are earning a paycheck doing what you enjoy, now there's a way to happiness!

Once you have outlined where your passions lie, answer these questions:

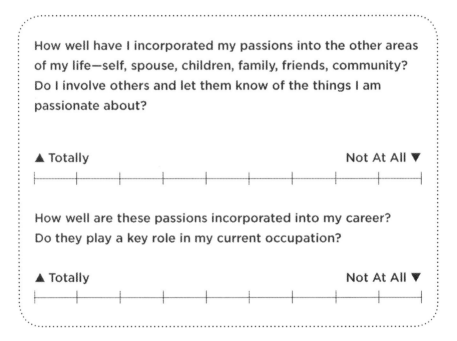

How well have I incorporated my passions into the other areas of my life—self, spouse, children, family, friends, community? Do I involve others and let them know of the things I am passionate about?

▲ Totally   Not At All ▼

How well are these passions incorporated into my career? Do they play a key role in my current occupation?

▲ Totally   Not At All ▼

If you can answer "totally" to both of the questions above, then you have achieved something that will help you tremendously in creating the life you want. And you should feel blessed that not only have you found something you are passionate about, but you have been able to blend that into your life, both at home and at the office.

Following Your Passions

Following your passions will bring so much more excitement and purpose to your life. Not only will it allow you to feel good about what you are doing, but it will also guarantee you that you are having an impact on those around you. When someone is passionate about what she is doing, it is contagious. It energizes all of the people around her and causes them to want to get onboard with something themselves. Further, if you fail to follow your passions, you will likely end up full of frustration and resentment. Abraham Maslow said, "A musician must make music, an artist must paint, a poet must write, if he is to be ultimately at peace with himself." Whatever your passion, you simply MUST do it. You must find a way to bring it into your life, both personally and professionally.

I have seen passion being brought into one's career play out countless times with perfection. As you may imagine, with my former career in the insurance and financial services industry, everyone we came across was *extremely* excited about sitting with us to discuss the possibility of dying prematurely or becoming sick or injured (not!) …people love being told of the need to save more to avoid going broke sometime during their retirement years! Are you kidding me? Most people ran screaming when they saw us coming. Why? Because, unfortunately, insurance and financial issues are something that many people don't like to face—thus, why it is imperative that they work with a knowledgeable professional to get them on the right track.

So, why would anyone want to go into the insurance business? Why would individuals subject themselves to this? The answer, quite simply, is because they have a passion for helping people. And the individuals in that industry who reach the highest levels of the profession let that *passion* be their driver. I saw many people come and go in that industry, and there was one certainty in each of them. The ones who were in it for themselves, not because of a passion for helping others, failed out of the business every time! While the ones who reached the pinnacle of success found joy each time they saw a client able to retire comfortably or send a child to college. They felt a sense of pride when they helped a client avoid financial ruin after the unexpected death of a spouse. These individuals had a passion for helping people … a passion that, having been molded into their careers, brought them a great deal of fulfillment and, as a byproduct, a great deal of success (monetarily and otherwise).

Another prime example of this is Oprah Winfrey. I must admit, I am a HUGE Oprah fan. I TiVo her show so that I can watch it when and if I happen to get a free minute during the evening (it's my guilty pleasure … but I have to confess, sometimes I catch Shaun shedding a tear too). Oprah epitomizes living with passion. One need only look at the joy on her face or the tears in her eyes during one of her "Angel" shows. She really loves what she is doing. Oprah not only has a passion for helping others, but also has put that passion to work in her numerous humanitarian efforts. What a tremendous role model for successful women. Having reached unparalleled levels of success herself, she still sees the value in continuing to follow her passion of helping others. Kudos to you, "Ms. O." Now if we can only get the rest of the female persuasion to follow their passions, imagine the impact we could have!

What type of impact can you make by following your passions? Think with me, for a moment, about the impact you feel you will have when you actively put your passion to work. What will you achieve? Write down how you envision your impact:

_____

_____

_____

_____

Now, read over what you have just written. Does it excite you? How great will you feel once you achieve this? Once you are following your passions and getting fulfillment out of every single day!

Living Out Your Passion in Your Life
Living out your passion is not as simple as saying, "I am passionate about _____, so now I'm gonna go make it happen." It would be nice if we could just uncover our passion and commit to follow it, but unfortunately it isn't quite that easy. We need to determine the steps we are going to take to live out this passion in our lives. It doesn't matter what your passion is.

The key to success is following that passion and taking steps every day to "live with passion" in your life.

Look back at what you listed as the things you are passionate about. As we go through the following chapters, I want you to keep these passions at the top of your mind. Refer to them often, as they will be key in creating the life you envision. When we talk about your career, look to bring passion into it. When we take a closer look at how you are spending your time, make sure you have allotted plenty of time to follow passionate pursuits.

If we can all work to bring more passion into our everyday lives, just imagine how fantastic a world it would be. It may sound simplistic, but if people can learn to mold their lives to incorporate their passionate pursuits, there would be less frustration and less contempt. There would be far fewer people blaming the world and the people in it for their problems and their unhappiness. I heard a great quote from Mark Twain (I'm sure you've figured out by now that I'm definitely a quote girl!) that said, "Don't go around saying the world owes you a living. The world owes you nothing. It was here first." Precisely! The world has nothing to do with the state of people's lives. If you don't like your life, change it. If you don't like your job, change jobs. And if you don't find passion in your life, uncover it … follow it … and live it!

CHECKLIST

○ Complete the following:
  "My passion is to _____

  _____

  _____

  _____ "

○ Outline how you plan to follow your passion.

○ Commit to bringing passion into the things you will do in your life (and remember this commitment as you continue your journey in the chapters that follow).

····· Chapter 4 ·····

GET YOUR CAREER IN GEAR

"Real success is finding your lifework in the work that you love"

— DAVID McCULLOUGH

WHAT IF THE STRENGTHS YOU HAVE JUST IDENTIFIED AND THE PASSION YOU HAVE UNCOVERED HAVE ABSOLUTELY NOTHING TO DO WITH YOUR CURRENT CAREER? What if the things that you have discovered bring you the greatest amount of fulfillment and excitement are not currently in your life? What now?

In this chapter, we are going to dig deeper and determine the changes that must be made to bring you closer to the life you envision for yourself. I promised at the beginning of this journey that you would have to make some changes and that some of them may be drastic. So hold onto your Spanx®, ladies, because here is where it starts to get tough!

Let's do a little check here. We've uncovered our unique gifts, and we've outlined and chosen to follow our passions. We have decided that we are *not* content with the state of our lives. We want more … we want to continue challenging ourselves to grow … and to live the life we've imagined.

Am I right?

To lead a strong, fulfilled life, we have to be willing to make some changes ... some drastic changes! Frequently, this means changes to the people you surround yourself with (which we will address in Chapter 6). Sometimes, it involves changes in the company you work for or in your career. I want you to look back at the strengths you outlined in Chapter 2 and review your passion statement from the last chapter as you answer these questions:

Does my current profession/position allow me to utilize my unique gifts?

○ Yes   ○ No

Are there other areas of my life where I am putting my strengths to good use?

○ Yes   ○ No

Am I living out my passion every day ... both at the office and at home?

○ Yes   ○ No

Does my career give me a sense of fulfillment? A sense that I am using my God-given talents in a way that I am proud of?

○ Yes   ○ No

If you did not answer unequivocally "yes" to each of these questions, I implore you to take a serious look at what you are doing for a living. Now when I say this, I am sure most of you are thinking, "This chic is nuts ... she's telling me to go out and be a nun ... and earn absolutely no money!" That is not at all what I am saying. In fact, I am hugely in favor of earning money ... and lots of it! If you are following your passions and doing with your life what you are truly put on this earth to do, you will earn money … in fact, you'll be rich … in more ways than just monetarily.

Part of the reason this book came to be is that I was sick of hearing friends and clients bitchin' and moaning about their careers and then doing *absolutely nothing* to change their circumstances. Waking up day in and day out and simply going through the motions. This has to end, ladies … and it has to end now! As a demographic, women are a hugely powerful group. And with the recent economic climate, we are becoming a more powerful and more important part of the workforce. We have strength in numbers, and it's about time we use that strength to help one another get ahead … and to get ahead by doing what we love and are good at.

There are countless examples of women who have followed their passions and, in doing so, created multimillion-dollar companies. These are women who sought to create a business out of the love and passion they had for their ideas, and who experienced tremendous amounts of success. Sara Blakely invented Spanx® out of her desire to create something comfortable that hid those awful panty lines. (I am certain you will all join me in saying, "Thank God for Sara!") Julie Aigner-Clark, the founder of The Baby Einstein Company (which I am sure all of us with young children have benefited from), didn't start out trying to make money—she just wanted to follow her passion of creating an educational product for her own child. Maxine Clark, founder of the Build-a-Bear Workshop chain, had no idea that her idea would be a runaway success—she just knew that kids love their teddies! Debbi Fields, the founder of Mrs. Fields cookies, and Discovery Toys' Lane Nemeth had no guarantees of success when they launched their businesses—they just followed their passions.

Ideas for how to turn your passion into a business are everywhere. Look for them. What about your passion could help others? Is there a business venture or a product in your head somewhere that could catch on? Think big; don't limit yourself. You never know where your idea could take you. Did these women know that their ideas would be huge successes when they started out? Likely not. I mean, who can really know that for sure? What they did have was passion and belief. *Passion* for what they were doing and *belief* that following that passion would put them on the right track.

Perhaps the entrepreneurial path isn't for you. Maybe you're a corporate girl or a 9-to-5'er. If that's the case, don't think you're getting off easy. The rules still apply. No matter your chosen profession, you need to have excitement and passion for it. Otherwise, it makes it pretty tough to get out of bed in the morning. Whether you are working for financial reasons, to fulfill your dreams, or simply to get out of the house for a while (admit it … some of you girls are working just to get a break from the kiddos!), working still makes up a huge part of our lives—and a huge part of our *selves*! If you continue to spend time doing something less than what you love, are good at, and are passionate about, there is no chance of building a better you!

You have to realize that every working mom out there has something unique to give … and to make this whole thing work, we have to show it to the world! Reminds me of another quote I came across. This one from my very favorite rock star. Not only is he über-talented, a writer of incredibly uplifting lyrics, and, let's face it, pretty easy on the eyes, he also has some words of wisdom for us all:

> "Each one of you has something no one else has, or has ever had:
> your fingerprints, your brain, your heart.
> Be an individual. Be unique. Stand out.
> Make noise. Make someone notice.
> That's the power of individuals."
> — JON BON JOVI

A number of you have already managed to incorporate your passions into your career—and big kudos to y'all. The challenge is to keep incorporating them, on a grander level. Be the best individual you can be. And together we'll create a force to be reckoned with. (Nothing can top a group of moms on a mission!)

For you corporate gals, look for opportunities to take on a project that lets you live your passion. If you have a passion for the environment, work to have your company sponsor Earth Day in your community. If you have a passion for helping others, agree to mentor the new girl who just started in the cubicle down the hall. Whatever your passion, look for additional ways to incorporate it into your career and your personal life.

If you are not a corporate exec or don't have a position in which you can call the shots, but are working in a 9-to-5 job, there are still numerous ways to incorporate your strengths and passions into your job. What are your unique gifts? And how can you use those gifts to bring added value to what you are doing? It doesn't take much. And that little bit extra goes a long way … and will benefit you in ways you never imagined.

Recently I read a story from the book *The Simple Truths of Service*, by Ken Blanchard and Barbara Glanz. The book was inspired by a story about "Johnny the Bagger," a grocery store bagger whom Ms. Glanz met after giving a corporate seminar for his supermarket chain. In the seminar, she empowered attendees to put their own personal stamp on their jobs to make their customers feel special. Johnny the Bagger did exactly that! An individual with Down syndrome and just under 20 years old, Johnny took his passion for wanting to make a difference and came up with a plan. Each evening after work, he came up with a "thought for the day." His dad helped him type up his quote on the computer. Johnny then printed copies, cut out each one, and signed his name on the back. The next day at the grocery store, he put one in each of his customers' bags. He used his gifts and created a special and unique experience for each person walking through his line.

But the story doesn't end there. Some weeks later, the manager noted that Johnny's line was significantly longer than any other checkout line in the store. When the manager attempted to get customers to move to a shorter line, they told him they preferred to wait … they were waiting for Johnny's "thought of the day." The impact that Johnny's sharing his gifts had on the store began to catch on. His co-workers began working to create special moments for their customers as well. The store's customer base grew, with customers visiting the store not just to pick up their groceries, but also for the special feeling they got from the passionate, empowered employees.

Each of us possesses unique gifts. Each of us has things we are passionate about. And when we share these with others, the impact will spread like magic!

What will you do to share your strengths and passions at work?

○   I can DO _____

○   I can SAY_____

○   I can HELP _____

○   I can OFFER _____

○   I can FEEL_____

If it seems like all we are doing is adding to your already long list of to-dos, nothing could be further from the truth. Instead of thinking of these items as additional things you need to do, I want you to begin to think of them as replacements for things you are already doing—things that do not bring you the same sense of passion and fulfillment. For example, in looking at committees to work on in your career, seek out those where you are able to most effectively lend your strengths and follow your passions. Be vocal about the projects you would like to work on and the tasks for which you would like to sign up. Don't stomp your feet and whine, "I wanna work on the children's hospital project." Rather, make your request known in a more powerful way by saying to your boss: "I have always had a passion for working on projects that improve the lives of children. And my strength and experience in working with hospital administrators make me a perfect pick to spearhead this project." What a powerful way to bring more passion into your career!

Be assured, when you come at it from a position of strength and actively seek to put your passionate side at the forefront, you (and those around you) will be astonished by all that you will accomplish.

Now, let's spend some time addressing those of you who answered a resounding "no" to the questions at the beginning of the chapter. It's time to get you started having some fun on the job! The next thing to ask yourself (and this can go for the women already living out their passions) is:

> Do I see any opportunity to incorporate the things I am passionate about into my current career?
>
> ○ Yes   ○ No

If you cannot answer "yes" to this question (let's hope this applies to only a few of you), you need to get out now! How can you expect to find fulfillment in a job for which you have NO excitement or passion? The answer is ... YOU CAN'T!

The greatest gift you can give yourself is to realize that you are at a dead end and that you must make a change. It may not be easy, but you need to begin to create your exit strategy. I do not advocate that you throw down your pen, shove back your chair, and walk out the door today (unless you can financially afford to do so), but I do advocate outlining your next steps. Think about what brings you excitement and fulfills your passions. And then think how you can work to create a career out of your passions. Most of the successful, passionate women I know had a few stops along their career path—none of them a complete waste of time. They all learned a few things that were useful to them later. With each of them, it wasn't until they were able to create careers where they could follow their passions that they truly found happiness.

I have worked hard over the years to continually mold my career and my position into one that utilizes my unique gifts and allows me to focus on the things I am passionate about. The road hasn't always been easy. It takes a conscious effort (and a good bit of change), but let me assure you ... it is well worth it.

If you are one of the lovely ladies who need to start from scratch, here are the steps to take. This will take some time, but don't despair. Things will happen for you, if you keep consciously focused and have the overriding goal of leading a more passionate, fulfilled life.

- List the ideas you have for careers or jobs that would allow you to live out your passions (whether corporate or entrepreneurial).
- Ask yourself, "What do I see myself ultimately doing as a career?"
- Research your new endeavor thoroughly. You don't have to be an expert from day one, but you do want to put yourself in a position to make educated decisions.
- Research these occupations to determine if you need any additional education or qualifications. And if so, develop a plan to obtain those qualifications.
- Determine if there is a market for or an opportunity within what you want to do.
- Determine the financial impact of your decision to make a career change. Will your new endeavor cover your financial obligations? Or will you need to dip into savings, take out a loan, or start your career on a part-time basis until it becomes financially feasible? Don't let finances keep you from doing what you need to do, but do have a clear understanding of how you will address this aspect.
- Talk to others with similar careers. What have been their struggles? Their successes?
- Build strong alliances with a variety of people—and with people whose strengths complement yours. Networking is key to this (and females make much more natural networkers than men).
- Outline the steps (with a timeline) for making a transition.
- Finally, ensure that you are combining your passion for your career with the passions in your life!

Big changes like this don't come easy. They take a lot of thought and preparation. Heck, so does raising children ... so I know you can do it! Be sure to share your challenges and successes with those around you; and through your entire transition, be sure to keep the overriding goal of a more passionate, fulfilled you at the tiptop of your mind. Philosopher and psychologist John Dewey said, "To find out what one is fitted to do, and to secure an opportunity to do it, is the key to happiness." My hope is that each and every one of you secures *your* opportunity and finds *your* own happiness!

Let's take a peek at what we accomplished in this chapter:

CHECKLIST

○ Identify if you are currently where you need to be in terms of your career and employer.
If not, what steps are you going to take?_____
_____
_____
_____.

○ What are the gifts I am going to incorporate into my career? How?_____
_____
_____
_____.

○ What passionate pursuits am I going to incorporate into my career? How? _____
_____
_____
_____.

····· **Chapter 5** ·····

THANK GOD FOR THE GPS

*"Any plan imperfectly executed is better than no
plan perfectly executed"*

— SCOTT SORRELL

**THIS CHAPTER IS ALL ABOUT MAPPING OUT YOUR
JOURNEY.** It focuses on having a plan that addresses the various
aspects of your life. Planning out your day, your week, your year. Planning
what your future will hold. What dreams you will realize. As capable
women, having accomplished much in your lives, you couldn't have made
it this far without some element of planning and visioning for the future.

In this chapter, we are going to develop a plan that encompasses
ALL areas of your life. Too many women (and men, for that matter) do an
excellent job of outlining their business goals yet fall very short in other
categories of their lives. We've all heard that you are much more likely to
achieve a goal once it is written down. Ask yourself: Do you consistently
write down *your* goals? For ALL areas of your life?

Your life—and the fulfillment you find in that life—is the grand
sum of all its parts. No single part can be ignored if you want to lead a
passionate and fulfilled life. It isn't possible to ignore *any* portion of your
life, because they are all ridiculously interdependent. You can't be fulfilled
in your career yet neglect your spouse or your kids. Consequently, you
can't lead a full life, despite how good things are when you walk through

the door at home, if you dread going to the office each day.

It is for this reason we see so many high-profile, powerful people who are completely miserable. Individuals at the top of their careers with horrible family lives. Individuals focusing all their attention on their kids while neglecting their spouse or their friends. How many CEOs do you know of who have gone through terrible divorces because they completely neglected their family lives? How many politicians and professional athletes have we seen make headlines when their mistresses (note the plural here!) are discovered? These things occur when people are lacking something in their lives—when some part of them is unfulfilled. When you are lacking in a particular area of your life, it is impossible to feel fulfilled. To truly lead a life of balance, purpose, and fulfillment, you need to take time to work on ALL of the parts that make up your life.

Over the years I have attended a number of seminars and read countless books that identified the need to focus on all facets of your life. And I thought I was doing so. I was conscious of the various areas of my life and was content, to varying degrees, with each of these areas. Had you asked me, I would have told you that I was actively paying attention to each of the areas. And that I was dedicating ample time to *every* one of them. I was soooooo wrong! Not only was I wrong, but I had no idea that I was even the least bit off base.

I paid some attention to each of the areas in my life; but until I was forced to take a closer look at how I was spending my time, I hadn't realized how truly out of alignment I was, and how I was virtually neglecting some key areas important in leading the fulfilled life I had always envisioned.

It's time for you to get your little fanny in gear and ensure you aren't neglecting any key pieces in your life.

To start, let's outline the key areas of a person's life. Areas you cannot and must not neglect. We're going to break this into seven areas: Self, Spouse, Children, Family, Career, Friends, and Community.

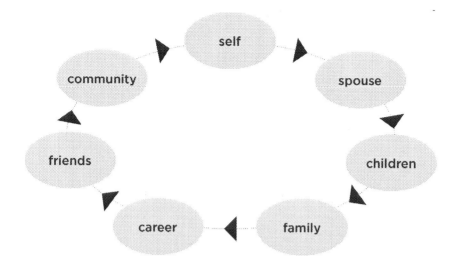

These areas are interrelated. They all exist alongside each other in a continual flow. Sometimes we may need to focus our time and energy more heavily in one particular area (as when we are having issues with a teenage child or going for a huge promotion at work). But the key that we must understand is that they ALL play a role and that NONE of them can be ignored. We need to work on each of the areas and ensure we are devoting adequate time to growing in ALL of these areas. As a quote by Greg Anderson reads: "Only one thing has to change for us to know happiness in our lives: where we focus our attention."

Take a look at the circle above. Where are you focusing your attention? Imagine the circle with one of the areas completely, or even partially, neglected—as if you drew a big red "X" right through that area. The normal flow of our lives would be disrupted. It would be impossible to find balance or fulfillment, because we weren't covering all the bases— we aren't focusing our attention on ALL the areas we need to.

Our challenge is to make sure we are covering all bases and are continually dedicating time and energy to each of these areas. To do so, let's outline the things you are already doing in regard to each of these areas. Start by listing (in the chart below) the things you do on a daily/ weekly/monthly basis for each of the following categories:

- Self (include things like manis/pedis, going to the gym, reading, hobbies)
- Spouse (include "date night" and scheduled "whoopee sessions")
- Children (what you do that is simply "mommy and me" time. This does NOT include the shuttle service you provide to and from practices and lessons … that's not really quality time!)
- Family (include loved ones aside from your spouse and children)
- Friends (include regular "girls' nights out" and getaway weekends. This could also include time on the phone catching up with old friends, or writing e-mails or letters to faraway friends just to stay in touch. Note: scheduled play dates where you wouldn't otherwise hang out with other mommies don't count!)
- Career (include time at the office and time spent on business travel. This should also include late-night report and presentation preparation—admit it … we all burn the midnight oil from time to time.)
- Community (include spiritual and religious pursuits and time and energy spent on charitable contributions)

Self	
Spouse	
Children	
Family	
Friends	
Career	
Community	

How even are your lists? Did you find that in one category you were able to just write and write, quickly filling up the entire space, while in another you had difficulty coming up with even one thing to jot down?

I wish I would have gone through an exercise like this years ago. Perhaps it would have let me address some of the "problem areas" in my life a bit earlier … before they grew into *real* problems! I would have found that while I took time for my daughter, and certainly devoted more than ample time and energy to my career, when it came to Shaun, myself, and my friends, I would have come up almost blank! As busy moms, the categories we tend to neglect most often are "Self" and "Friends." Even today, I have to consciously pay attention to all of the areas of my life to ensure I am nurturing each of them on a consistent basis.

So, how do your lists look? Are you devoting time to each of these critical areas (while still tending to all the 17 million other things on your to-do list!)? Let's talk a bit about the areas many of us neglect. And what you can do about them.

Think for a minute about the friends in your life. Are they true friends? People you spend time with on a regular basis discussing things that matter? Things of importance? Are they, without question, confidantes in your life with whom you can share your greatest secrets and your most difficult challenges? With many women, this just isn't the case. They have a group of friends they "hang out with," but few true confidantes. As you go through this exercise, work on creating activities that allow you to spend time cultivating *true* friendships—not the superficial ones we see too often in society. With today's transient society, where people frequently move from city to city and state to state, it's no wonder this category tends to suffer for a bunch of us. My challenge to you is to not let that happen. If you have lived in the same town all your life, you have no excuse. And, if you are like me and have moved around a bit, don't think I am letting you off the hook—do some work, find like-minded people you connect with, and work to develop those relationships in your life.

The other category where many women draw a virtual blank is "Self." Like most "workaholic moms" out there, many of us spend the majority of our time and energy on work and family. The problem with that (and the problem many of you are facing) is this: not only are you missing out on a wealth of fun and fulfillment, you are also not allowing yourself to become a whole person, a whole *fulfilled* person. And in doing so, you aren't bringing your best self to those around you. Until I completed the above exercise and put it down on paper, I had absolutely NO idea I was so out of whack! And I didn't realize I was neglecting one of the very areas that would make me a more well-rounded, complete person. (I'll give you some fun ideas that will help you address the area of "Self" later in the "Mom's Going for a Drive" chapter.)

When you don't take time to cultivate ALL areas of your life, your life is lacking. You aren't a complete person. And you will suffer for it. This suffering is only the beginning of huge problems that can unfold. Let me share with you a few more details on how my lack of attention in certain areas of my life almost cost me everything I cherished. As I mentioned, I had my share of difficulties and lived way too long in a negative state of mind—where I was a miserable, disillusioned crazy woman (can anyone relate?). At the time, I was unable to see how neglecting some of the seven key areas had contributed to the situation I created.

It was many years ago, toward the beginning of my career in the financial services industry, and I was throwing everything I had into my career. I went in early for meetings, stayed late, and frequently worked nights. I got to be great friends with a number of the other advisors in the office and spent a great deal of time with them outside the office as well. I was having some early successes in the career and liked how I was doing career-wise. I would drop the little one off at day care in the morning (I had only one child at the time) and was usually there to kiss her good night when she went to bed. Shaun and I didn't take time to do anything for just the two of us, and truthfully I really had very few friends outside the office (which I see all too often with career women today).

I was pretty happy ... or so I thought. Yet the longer I went down that road, the more miserable I became. I began spending even more time at the office and spent virtually no time with any of my friends. And, what's worse, I wasn't engaged in the relationships I had at home. Over time I had gradually begun to neglect the two people most important to me in my life ... my husband and my child. I was not actively working to cultivate those relationships. Hell, I wasn't actively working to cultivate anything except work.

I was living in a state of denial. A state where I "thought" things were great and that I was doing everything I should be doing. Over time, things in my life began to fulfill me less and less. I began to dislike my career. I hated the city we lived in and loathed being away from my own family. I was angry with what I felt was a lack of contribution by Shaun to our family, both emotionally and financially. And I blamed my lack of friends on not having time for anything other than work. Does any of this resonate in *your* life?

So what did all of that complaining and self-loathing get me? It got me the *absolute worst year of my entire life.* My productivity at work sharply declined—despite the fact that I was still spending countless hours in the office (mostly to avoid being at home). I began to resent Shaun and blamed him for all of the things going wrong in my life. I wasn't actively working on cultivating any relationships … except with the few people who, I felt, led the life I wanted to lead—the life of a single career person, who from my naïve eyes seemed to "have it all" (i.e., a solid career, with few stresses outside the office!).

I got to a point where I *thought* the only way for me to truly "have it all" was to start over and be single! It was totally irrational, but as screwed up as my head was at that point, I thought that was what I wanted. (Have any of you ever gotten to that point in your relationship?) So, that summer, Shaun and I separated for a bit. We remained on amicable terms and saw each other every day (so that we were both there to tuck Bailey in at night), and we went to counseling to try to talk through and work out our problems. I knew that I loved him very deeply; but I was so messed up about what I wanted out of my life, it was insane. After a few months apart, we knew that what we had was too special to abandon and we chose to continue to work through things … under the same roof. It was a long and very difficult journey, but one well worth traveling. We came out of it stronger as a couple and with a newfound commitment to making our lives work … for both of us.

What it boiled down to was this: neither of us owned up to the things we were doing that contributed to our downward spiral. We weren't taking ownership of the choices we were making to be less than we could be. We weren't working individually or collectively, as a team, on each of the seven areas outlined above. We were letting life "happen" to us instead of taking control of our futures and our destinies. We were choosing to *react* to our circumstances instead of shaping our own future.

You see, awhile before our troubles began, Shaun had unexpectedly lost a very dear friend and had a great deal of trouble coping with this. He lost a lot of his drive and enthusiasm and suffered from a great deal of depression. At the same time, I was selfishly involved in my career (pay attention, all you moms who seem to spend 24-7 at the office!). I was not actively spending time cultivating *our* relationship, and I was oblivious to the fact that I should be helping him through this (remember, at that time my "Spouse" column was pretty empty). I was too heavily invested in the "Career" column and WAY too light everywhere else. Likewise, Shaun was heavily invested in "Children" and "Friends," yet took little time to work on "Self" and to address any of the issues that were slowly brewing in the "Spouse" category. Not only were we both neglecting areas critical to our happiness, and to our success as a family, but we were WAY out of alignment with each other. And had NO idea what was happening until things were already way out of whack.

Fortunately for us, we were able to recognize and address our issues before it was too late. Before we had abandoned the opportunity to have an incredible relationship. We CHOSE to work through our issues. And we actively put everything we had into making our lives better.

I could not imagine what my life would be like had we not gotten our butts into gear and decided to work things out (not to *wait* for things to work themselves out). Wherever you are lacking in your life … whichever category above needs cultivating … it will not improve by your sitting on your arse and doing nothing. It takes owning up to the fact that you have been a slacker in that area. It takes attention … the right type of attention. And it takes commitment to make that category something that will bring a sense of fulfillment to your life. It doesn't work to be fulfilled in two or three areas and not the rest. You have to address them all.

Let's claim what is ours … happiness and contentment in EVERY area of our lives. And let's begin by focusing on the areas that need work (without neglecting the others).

In which of the seven areas do you feel you are doing a GREAT job?

* _____
* _____
* _____
* _____
* _____

Which areas have some work to be done?

* _____
* _____
* _____
* _____
* _____

For you to make these areas work, you must find a place for each of them in your life. There needs to be time devoted to all seven of them. Hours spent cultivating each category. The hours don't have to be equal, but you do need to address each category. It's OK that one area consumes more of your time than others. It's YOUR life. Too often we spend way too much time trying to act the way we "think" we are supposed to act or saying the things we "think" we should say. In prioritizing these categories, don't lie to yourself because you think it "sounds good." If something isn't as important, it isn't as important. Don't try to force it into being so.

Look back over the areas you listed above as needing work. I would bet money (and I am not the betting kind) that you aren't investing enough in those areas. Sure, you might do a charity fundraiser here and there. Or take the kids to your place of worship on special occasions. You might even have "date night" once every three or four months. But aside from that, you aren't doing squat! So, for all you busy gals, we are going to do what we do when we need to get things done. We are going to *schedule* the time to do it! We're going to plot all of those categories into our cute little day planners and make the effort to cultivate these areas in our lives. And the coolest thing is … YOU get to create your own degree of "balance"!

In order to determine where we will fit these into our busy calendars, we must first determine which of these areas is most important to us. Take each of the seven categories and rank them in the order of importance. Remember, there is no right or wrong answer here. Rank them in the order of importance to you (not to your spouse, not to your boss, but to YOU). I *will* comment on the fact that when I ask most women to rank these categories, they often rank themselves last. Not that there is anything wrong with that. I simply want you to think about it and consider, for once, not always putting yourself *dead last*. How good can you expect to be for others when you don't take care of Y-O-U?

Rank the categories … in order of importance to you (Self, Spouse, Children, Family, Friends, Career, and Community)?

Rank the categories... in order of importance to you (Self, Spouse, Children, Family, Friends, Career, and Community)?

#1 _____

#2 _____

#3 _____

#4 _____

#5 _____

#6 _____

#7 _____

You likely didn't rank "Career" as the No. 1 thing of importance in your life (unless, of course, your boss is reading over your shoulder), but I do realize that the vast majority of your waking hours, at least during the workweek, are spent in this category. For this reason, we are going to start by plugging the hours you work into your calendar. Regardless of where you ranked "Career," I want you to **enter your "ideal" work hours in the schedule that follows.** If you work a flexible schedule or travel frequently, plug in what you would like your typical hours to be, knowing that these will frequently change and that you will often slot other categories right in the middle of your day. We are creating an "ideal" schedule here … not a "you must adhere exactly or die" schedule.

I know we all wish we could work four hours a day. And for some of you, that may be possible. If so, put 'em in there. I want you to create an "ideal" for yourself. Something to work toward each and every week. A friend and business coach once told me that "our work expands or contracts to fit the time you have for it." What a great statement. And so very true. For the most part, we get our work done in the hours we make for it. If we focus our energies on being *efficient* while we are at the office, we will be able to take time for the other areas of our lives … those that likely rank more important. This is what will lead us to a more fulfilled life.

Too often I see people wasting time in their day (and I am not just talking about the "death by meeting" that most corporations are guilty of). Look at your day and actively work to see where you could save a few minutes here and there. In my own business, I have found that the simple act of shutting my office door actually frees me up about an hour a day! It sounds trivial, but you cannot imagine the massive number of "Hey, have you got a minute?" meetings and conversations I avoid by closing the door to my office.

As unfair as it is, as professional women we frequently become the "mom" of the office (especially in more male-dominated industries). People come to us for everything—"Where should my spouse and I go for dinner?" or "I've got this terrible cold" … let me tell you all about it as I spread my germs all around your office! We somehow become the resident expert in things that don't really matter to the life of our business, and people act as if we are there to be some type of personal concierge. What's worse, as the sweet accommodating mom types we are, we actually take time out for them! ARE YOU KIDDING ME? If you want to have time to cultivate each of the seven critical areas in your life, you have to guard your time. You have to make choices about where you spend it. Time is a precious resource. The next time the guy down the hall comes to you to tell you all about the monster truck rally he attended with his son, I want you to realize that you are letting this take up time you could be spending on YOU … or on *anyone* else for that matter!

This process won't come without difficulty. Since I created my own "ideal schedule," it has been a HUGE challenge to stick to it. There is rarely a week that goes by that shakes out exactly as I have outlined it. That's not the point of this exercise. The point is to make you *prioritize* the various areas of your life. And, more importantly, that you make them ALL fit into your schedule— on a regular basis. As you heard in my story (and have perhaps encountered on your own), neglecting any of the categories can cause you to suffer and perhaps lose something you cherish. You will never lead as fulfilled a life as you could without devotion to each of these areas. Once you prioritize these categories in your own life, you know where you would ideally like to spend your time. It isn't always possible, but it sure as heck makes it easier to CHOOSE where to devote your time and energies. There will still be challenges and conflicts, but you will be clear where your priorities lie. And more conscious of making sure you take time for all the pieces of your life … and not just spend time on the fires that need to be put out.

Whenever you are faced with a choice of how to spend your time, go back to how you ranked the seven categories. For me personally, I rank "Children" ahead of "Career," so when Bailey asks me to serve as a chaperone on a school field trip, it's a no-brainer. I schedule my work around it. And I make no excuses about the fact that that is where I will be for those four or five hours. My co-workers know and my clients know. At first I thought I would be seen as not able to hang with the big boys or as being on a trip down the infamous "mommy track," but I have not found that to be the case at all. I have found that people respect me for my decisions. Sure, there are some that might look down on the fact that I left work to go on a field trip. Or that I wasn't available for a late-night meeting because it conflicted with a dance recital. But honestly, do I care what these people think? Am I going to waste my time worrying what these people, who have no bearing on my life whatsoever, really think of my choices? Of course not. *They* aren't on my priority list, so why should they enter into my decision-making process? We can't please everyone all of the time, and it will frustrate us if we try.

Unfortunately, in many companies, there still exists the double standard that, as a mom, when you leave work for a child-related reason, you are looked at sideways; yet, when your male counterpart does the same, he is applauded for being an involved father. It's bogus … it's insane … but it happens! Don't waste energy on it—just focus on the people you care most about. Make your priorities known to your family, your friends, and those with whom you work. Therefore, they aren't surprised by any of the choices you make. Bring your whole self to the office and your whole self home. And never feel like you need to apologize for how you choose to spend your time. You are living within your values and sticking to what allows you to live the best, most fulfilled life possible, *for you*! More importantly, despite the hours you may work, or the insane amount of passion and dedication you have toward what you do professionally, your children won't doubt for a millisecond that they are a MUCH higher priority in your life!

How will you spend your time so that the people in your life know they are a priority? By now you should have already filled in your ideal work hours—so you can cross "Career" off the list. Next, I want you to start at the top of you priority list and one by one add those items to your schedule. Pencil in church and community obligations. Jot down those exercise classes you take (or that you need to get your butt off the couch and sign up for). Include "date nights," books clubs, one-on-one time with the kiddos. Don't forget anything. And don't forget to include something for each of the categories. There may be some things that you want to schedule on less than a weekly basis, and that is perfect. (Lord knows, as much as we'd like a twice-weekly "girls' night out," we're not as young as we used to be and we probably would lose a little productivity at the office!) For those items, include them on the "regular basis" list.

	Sun.	Mon.	Tues.	Wed.	Thurs.	Fri.	Sat.
5 am							
6 am							
7 am							
8 am							
9 am							
10 am							
11 am							
12 pm							
1 pm							
2 pm							
3 pm							
4 pm							
5 pm							
6 pm							
7 pm							
8 pm							
9 pm							
10 pm							
11 pm							

Other items to include on a regular basis

Now that you know how you would ideally like to spend your time, how the heck are you going to do it? To start, let the people in your life know they are a priority. Share with them how you intend to spend your time, and let them know how you plan to incorporate them into your schedule. Then watch as *they* start holding you accountable to your newfound dedication to addressing EACH of these areas of your life.

Sure, you'll fall off the wagon sometimes, but the key is that you continually work to incorporate each of these critical areas into your life. One of the ways you can do this is to make sure you address each of these areas when you are doing your goal planning. As professionals, we are all accustomed to outlining our monthly, quarterly, and annual goals. At least I hope so, or your business is on an express trip down the toilet! But ask yourself this: When you outline your goals, is it all business? Do you regularly include your personal goals in your planning?

○ Yes   ○ No

If so, you're on the right track. Take time to review your goals and ensure you have at least one goal that addresses *each* of the seven categories outlined above. The only way to fully ensure you cultivate all of these areas is to create goals around them and then execute on those goals. If you are among the majority who has put only your business goals to paper, I want you to take this opportunity to go a step further. We have all heard that we are much more likely to achieve our goals when we put them to paper. And that is precisely what we are going to do here.

Since changing my goal planning to incorporate each of the seven areas of my life, I have found that I think harder about the things I really want to accomplish and that I don't let those things slide. I have something to work toward throughout the year in *each* of the areas of my life. If I didn't, I'd probably focus on all the "token" goals: increase business revenue 20 percent, recruit ten new associates, lose 10 pounds (I swear that one makes the list every year!). You should not only have business goals, but also have ones that really put a smile on your face. Ones that force you to think bigger and get more out of your life. Commit to achieve more than you have ever imagined ... in ALL areas of your life. Think big. Envision what you will accomplish in the coming days ... years

… decades! It all starts with that first step. In order for you to transform your life, you have to decide what steps you are going to take to make that transformation. As a starting point, outline at least one goal for each of the seven categories we identified—a goal you will achieve within the next twelve months.

My Goals for the Next Twelve Months

Self: _____

_____

Spouse: _____

_____

Children: _____

_____

Family: _____

_____

Friends: _____

_____

Career: _____

_____

Community: _____

_____

Now that you have taken this critical first step, make it a practice to continue along this path every time you create goals. Each time you do a goal-planning session at work (which should be done, at a minimum, annually), outline goals for each of the other six areas. Use your accountability partner to keep you in check. Share your goals with your spouse and your children. Believe me, if your goal is to take the kids to Disneyland before the end of the year, you have just found the absolute best people to hold you accountable! You are much more likely to achieve your goals when you put some butts in the stands to cheer you on and to keep you on track (we'll talk more about your personal cheering section in the next chapter).

Goal setting is critical to your success in leading a full life. It is impossible to come anywhere close without clearly defined, tangible goals. In addition, these goals need to continue to challenge you to grow, to push you to be the best that you can be. When you are setting your goals each year … think BIG … think HUGE!

One of the ways to help you do this is to develop your **"100 Things to Do Before I Die"** list. I created this list for myself, at the suggestion of one of my mentors, when I was a new associate. When first presented with the task, I thought it sounded fun, and pretty easy. I quickly found it to be anything but. It was tough. To be able to identify 100 things you would like to accomplish in your lifetime is a pretty big task. The first forty or fifty items are pretty easy to come up with. Beyond that, you really have to stretch your mind—to think bigger than you have ever thought before. To envision yourself accomplishing things beyond your wildest dreams. It probably took me a month to outline my "100 Things to Do." Since then, there has been no stopping me. I have already accomplished more than a quarter of the things on my list—most of those being things that were well beyond my wildest imagination when I developed the list.

That is precisely the goal with this exercise. Just as it did for me, I want this exercise to cause you to think bigger. To envision accomplishing things you never imagined. Then, go after these goals with fervor. *Refer to the "100 Things to Do Before I Die" appendix in the back of the book and create your very own "100 Things" list.*

Once your list is complete, keep it in front of you. Review it regularly, as you should do with your monthly/quarterly/annual goals. Once you complete an item on your list, highlight it (but don't remove it). Over time it will feel great to see all that you have accomplished. From time to time, you will find that an item on your list no longer energizes you. Take it off the list, but be sure to replace it with a new goal. The list should be a source of excitement—full of things you look forward to accomplishing. It should be something you share with others. As I do with all of my goals, I shared my list with Shaun, and he is as excited about the list as I am. He is continually searching for ways I can cross something off my list.

A couple of years ago, we were on vacation in Anguilla with a group of associates (gorgeous place—I absolutely recommend it!). We were having a blast and I got to mark "visit the Caribbean" off my list, so I was quite the happy camper. But Shaun did me one better and helped me cross two more items off my list. As a surprise, he signed me up to go "swimming with the dolphins." It was something that had been on my list since I created it, but I had not yet had the opportunity to do. When one of our friends mentioned they were going, Shaun immediately signed me up. It was awesome! I have to admit that I was completely scared out of my gourd at first. To give you a little insight, I am not what you would call an "animal person." Most of them scare the ever-loving poop out of me! So, despite the fact that I was psyched to go and had been waiting years to cross this off my list, I was still freaking out when I got into the tank. But once I took some deep breaths and realized that the sweet little dolphins were, in fact, not going to eat me for dinner, I was fine. In fact, I couldn't wipe the grin off my face (and I have the pictures to prove it). Checking things off my list didn't stop there on this trip. I was actually able to cross a third thing off my list on this trip: "Go snorkeling."

This particular item was one that challenged me even more than swimming with the dolphins. When I made the list, I thought it sounded like a fun and exciting thing to do. Swimming out in the ocean with creatures of the sea! Well, as my daughter would say ... OMG! I thought I was going to die! Truthfully, before I even left the boat, I was ready to chicken out. And, were it not for the fact that I had put it on my "100 Things" list, I probably would have. I guess that I had not fully thought through the whole "jumping in the ocean with wild creatures and swimming around a barrier reef ... far away from the safety of our boat" thing when I put this grand idea on my list. But, nonetheless, I was there and I was not going to chicken out. After all, Shaun and several of our friends were there with me, and they all seemed fine with the idea. So what did I do? I jumped in the water and went.

In all fairness, I must admit that from the moment I was in the water I was sizing up the competition. I knew barracudas were known to be in the area, so from the start I began looking around at who in the group was larger than me (and would likely make a more filling meal for any would-be predators!). Our snorkeling guide, who noticed how terrified I was, offered to take my arm and guide me through the expedition. Of course, I had my strong, protective husband with me, but hell, I'm no fool, and this guy had experience in these waters. So I let Shaun and the rest of the group follow closely behind as I stayed attached to the one person I knew could safely navigate us on our journey! And ... I am still alive to tell the tale!

Sometimes we are afraid to go after our goals. We have fears of failing—whether these fears are rational or irrational (like my being eaten by a shark). And, when this happens, the key is to line up our resources (in my case the snorkeling guide) and tackle our fears head-on. We wouldn't have put something down as a goal if it weren't important to us. And it wouldn't be a worthwhile goal if it weren't laced with some challenges. It is in moments like these that we have to keep charging forward. These are the moments that shape our future. The moments when we *choose* to move forward in spite of what we fear. This is precisely why I am empowering you to think beyond the present and envision all the things the future can hold for you.

Having my "100 Things" list has empowered me to try things I wouldn't otherwise try. To keep going when I was scared and ready to give up. And to reach for goals I thought to be impossible. One of the things I wrote on my list the very first time I worked on it was to write a book (and to make the *New York Times* best-seller list). At the time, I had never even thought of writing a book, much less what it would be about. But fast-forward almost a decade, and here we are. In my eyes, the list gives you an opportunity to dream. To put to paper the things that lie dormant at the back of your mind. Things that will eventually take you from being a good person who has accomplished a lot to being an exceptional person who leads a life of passion, power, and purpose! My goal for you is that you create a road map to that exceptional life. And that you have (at least) "100 Things" to help you get there!

You've accomplished a lot so far on the journey through this book ... and we're just getting started! In the next chapter, we're going to spend some time making sure you have the right people along for the ride (and spend time talking about how to rid yourself of the ones who aren't). But first, let's make sure the GPS is working and we've mapped out our path to greatness.

CHECKLIST

○ Outline how you are spending your time.

○ Prioritize the seven key areas of your life.

○ Develop your "ideal" schedule.

○ Write down one goal for each category that you will accomplish in the next twelve months.

○ Create your "100 Things to Do Before I Die" list.

· · · · · **Chapter 6** · · · · ·

FINDING THE RIGHT TRAVEL COMPANIONS

"Success, in business as well as in life, is directly dependent on the quality of people you surround yourself with."

— PAUL HICKEY

HOW MANY OF YOU FEEL THERE IS SOMEONE, OR PERHAPS A NUMBER OF PEOPLE, STANDING BETWEEN YOU AND WHAT YOU REALLY WANT OUT OF LIFE? How many of them are people close to you? I am here to tell you those people aren't standing in your way at all. Rather, you are *allowing* them to stand there!

There comes a day when you have to put an end to this. To refuse to let others stand in your way. Guess what, girls? That time is now! It's time to forge your own way. To stand up to the people telling you that you can't do something—whether they are telling you directly or indirectly—and say, "Shape up or ship out!" It's time you realize the people you surround yourself with have a huge impact on who you are and where you go with your career and your life. Each of us needs people in our cheering sections, people to pat us on the back when we do well and dust us off and send us back out there when we fall down.

I was fortunate to grow up with parents and a brother who encouraged me by saying that anything was possible. I was taught that I should go for whatever it was that I wanted in life. I realize that not everyone is that fortunate. Some of you are used to people telling you why you can't accomplish something. Why you will never be a CEO or own your own business. I am here to tell you that you can—you can do *whatever* you set out to do in life. Not only that, but I am here to tell you that in order to climb the ladder of success in your cute little Jimmy Choos, you have to distance yourself from any naysayers. In this chapter, we are going to discover how.

Having the right people in your life is imperative to creating the life you want. If you aren't currently surrounded by the right people, now is the time to make a change. If you don't do it soon, there is a new generation of working women coming up who are convinced the world is theirs. They believe nothing can stand in their way. And if you don't watch out, in a few years they're gonna climb right past you on the ladder to the top. Don't believe me? Ask any 'tween what they want to be when they grow up, and listen as they regale you with their grandiose dreams. Ask them what they are most concerned about, and they'll likely say the environment. Kids today think about things aside from what's on television and dream things well beyond what we dream of. They are convinced they can do everything they dream of and plan on doing exactly that.

My eleven-year-old, Bailey, is already pursuing charitable as well as entrepreneurial endeavors. And she has every intention of being president of the United States (after brief stints as an artist and a pop star). She's already picked out where she is going to college … Harvard (we better spice up our college fund!). Then she plans to attend law school! Don't get me wrong—I am extremely proud of the fact that she is so driven and has already given thought to how she plans to contribute to the world around us. And, if you actually met my daughter, you'd be convinced she may do ALL of it. But really? She's ELEVEN!

When I was her age, the thing I was most concerned about was not catching "cooties" from the boys in my class. Whatever happened to cooties? They seem to have disappeared. Kids today are different—they grow up faster. And while we need to be careful to allow them to still be kids (which I will address later in the book), we also need to realize that these children will be hitting the workforce in another decade, and we need to make sure we have created our own fulfilling, balanced lives long before they get there. The Gen Yers and the Millennials demand flexibility in their careers and the ability to take time for themselves—and they are getting it. Why not grab a piece of that action for ourselves?

When we were younger, we thought we could (and would) have it all. So what happened? Who put it in our minds that we could climb only so high? That there were limits to what we could accomplish? That we couldn't effectively juggle a busy, high-profile career with a booming family?

Take a serious look at where you are in your life. You're a working mom. Needless to say, you have had your share of accomplishments. But have you gone as far as you wanted? Have you reached your dreams? If you had, you wouldn't have even picked up a copy of this book ... there's got to be something you are still longing for!

When did you decide to limit yourself? To become less than your God-given talents allow you to be? Who are you listening to that's holding you back from your dreams? It is imperative that you get a grasp on the fact that the direction of your life is up to YOU. From this moment on, I want you to take control of where that direction is leading you.

We are going to work through an exercise to determine *who* may be in the way of creating the life you want, and also develop a plan to attack the issue.

It should go without saying that each of us needs to limit the time we spend with people who are negative influences in our lives. Just as we learned as teenagers, we should stay away from "bad influences." We all know this. We've all grown up being told this (heck, we've told it to our own children). Why, then, do you have bad influences in your life? The answer is that you've *invited* them in. You have allowed them to enter and remain a part of your life. Not only that, but you have allowed them to have a direct impact on where your life is headed. We're not talking about the drug-dealing, shoplifting influences — God knows we should have the sense to stay away from them. We're talking about the people who by their words or actions are keeping you from becoming the person you could be. The ones holding you back from the life you desire.

There is only one reason these people hold you back ... because you let them. This has to stop, and it has to stop now! If you find yourself falling victim to this trap, let's work to end it today! How do you do this?

In concept, it is actually quite simple ... you absolutely REFUSE to let *anyone* keep you down (easier said than done, right?).

Let's start by listing all the people you feel are standing in the way of your success. Who are the people in your life you are *allowing* to keep you from the life you desire? This could be co-workers or bosses, friends or family members, or even the people closest to you. Anyone you feel, who by words or actions or even by lack of support for the things you are doing, is holding you back.

Name these people:

_____ _____
_____ _____
_____ _____

Describe these people:

_____
_____
_____

Describe how you feel when you are around these people:

_____
_____
_____
_____

Now, answer this question: Why the hell are you allowing these people to remain as suppressors in your life? Why are you letting them hold you back and keep you from living the best life possible? I am going to tell you something that I hope stays with you indefinitely: *you teach people how to treat you.* If you allow them to zap your energy, they will. If you listen when they tell you that you "can't" accomplish something, that is exactly what will happen. It's inevitable—you have just given them permission. As Mark Twain instructed, "Keep away from people who try to belittle your ambitions. Small people always do that, but the really great make you feel that you, too, can become great."

I am not suggesting that you completely alienate yourself from key people in your life. Instead, if you feel these people are holding you back, you need to work to make them your advocates. With how many of these people have you shared your dreams? Have you told them where you plan to go and how you plan to get there? If they truly care for you and have your best interests at heart, they will want to see you succeed; they may even be able to help you chart a course to get there. On the other hand, if you share your dreams with them and they begin with the laundry list of why you will never be able to accomplish these things, then … it's time to surround yourself with a new group of people.

I want you to refer back to the people you listed as standing between you and your goals. What do you plan to do to get them on board with your vision? Make time to talk to each person on this list, catch up on things, and share *your* goals and plans with them. Ask them what *they* want their life to look like. If they are encouraging and receptive to learning more (and don't give you a zillion reasons why things aren't working out for them), bring 'em along for the ride. Help them learn how *they* can grow and create the life *they* desire.

Capture what you will say and do below:

_____

_____

_____

The truth is, when you talk to these people, there will inevitably be someone who refuses to get on board. There will be someone, and it may be someone very close to you, who does absolutely nothing but complain about her situation—or gives you a laundry list of why things probably won't happen for you. It will hurt, but the key is that you don't let these people drag you down to their level of discontent. You can't expect them to relish in your successes and your vision for the future when they feel lousy about their own situation. So, what are you to do with these relationships? The answer is: you keep them (as long as they aren't toxic or abusive), but you MUST change the dynamic of the relationship. In all of your interactions with these individuals, you must work to ensure the focus stays on the positive and they don't lead you into a discussion clouded with negativity.

Growth is tough, and often we find that we outgrow some of the relationships that have been dear to us for so long. It is our job to encourage and empower these friends and loved ones to grow along with us. But, with that said, you have to be willing to cut your losses if they refuse to grow. I am not saying change your phone number and never speak to them again. But you have to be clear that if you are to continue moving forward and growing, the dynamic of the relationship with the people holding you back has to change.

Throughout my life, I was fortunate to have a number of friends. I grew up in a midsize town in Georgia, where the majority of my friends stayed put after college. Or, if they did venture outside our great little city, it was only a few hours away. When I made the choice to move out of state to be with my future husband, I left a lot of them behind. Most were surprised that I was moving away. Some even told me it was a bad decision. Yet I knew it was the right thing for me to do. It was a move toward creating the life I wanted. At the time, I would have sworn that I would not lose contact with anyone. Today, aside from casual contact via social media sites, there are only a few people from my childhood and college years whom I remain close friends with. And I have chosen those few wisely. I maintain contact with the ones who give me energy when I talk to them. Who continue to challenge and encourage me. Those whom I truly want to be a part of my life. Some of the people I surrounded myself with while younger, I simply outgrew. It wasn't that I was any better than them personally, professionally, or financially. I was just at a different stage, pursuing different goals and different interests. I still speak with some of them on occasion; they are just not part of my inner circle. The relationships are still there—the dynamic of them has just changed.

While you may still maintain some contact with people who have been part of your life for so many years, the core of a number of those relationships has most likely changed. The change is often hard to see when you're in the midst of it. You don't wake up one day and say, "Well, this is different." Rather, some of your relationships just stay status quo. Nonetheless, it is important to take stock of *all* the relationships in your life to best determine the ones to cultivate as well as the ones you need to examine a bit more closely to see if they are toxic to your creating the life you desire.

The bottom line in assessing your current relationships is that if you don't feel energized when you're around these people, you don't need them (or at the very least, you need to minimize the time you spend with these energy zappers). Don't be fooled—this will be hard. It will be downright awful to let go of some of these relationships. However, you may have to do just that. Regardless of how long these people have been in your life, or what they may have meant to you in the past, you have to do the best thing for you. There are plenty of other people out there to encourage, motivate, and challenge you. What is most important is what we put into the relationships we *choose* to continue—the ones that feed and challenge us to grow.

There is a plethora of people out there to support each of us. Some are in your life now; others you've yet to meet. Your challenge is to find those people. Whose mere presence lifts your spirits? Who in your life makes you think you can accomplish anything you set out to do? These are the people you *have to* spend time with. The more of these relationships you have, the more success you will enjoy, and the easier it will be to create the life you desire.

As Paul Hickey said at the beginning of the chapter: "Success, in business as well as in life, is directly dependent on the quality of people you surround yourself with." It is imperative that you keep this top of mind at all times. If you want to live a nutritious life, surround yourself with nutritious people. Likewise, if you surround yourself with energy zappers, your energy *will* be zapped. If you choose to keep close to you people who continually tell you why you can't move to the next level, you will subconsciously listen, and you will stay exactly where you are ... and not a step beyond!

Visualize yourself standing on a huge stage in the middle of a jampacked theater, curtain drawn (for the sake of this exercise, we will assume that all fears of public speaking that you may have are nonexistent!). The emcee recites your numerous accolades, in preparation for your acceptance of a "Lifetime Achievement Award." He rattles off your list of accomplishments (which, of course, includes a TON of things from your "100 Things" list). The curtain opens, to the roar of applause, and you look out into a sea of smiles and cheers. All people there to celebrate your accomplishments. All people who have helped you along your journey. What faces do you see in the crowd? Who are the nutritious people in your life? Who makes you feel you can conquer any mountain? Who is always there to provide encouragement and challenge? List these individuals (or organizations) below:

In contrast to the naysayers you outlined earlier, describe how these people make you feel:

Let's take it a step further. Who else do you want in your life? Are there any people you want to add to your team (a mentor, a coach)? People you want on your team who could open some doors for you? Are there any organizations you feel you should join to meet more like-minded, driven women?

> **What else do you want in your life?**
>
> _____
>
> _____
>
> _____
>
> _____
>
> **What is your plan to reach out to these people and make them members of your support team?**
>
> _____
>
> _____
>
> _____
>
> _____

You can't do this alone. We've all heard the expression "Behind every good man, there's a good woman." Don't you think the same holds true for us? Behind every good working mom climbing the ladder of success is a whole cheering section! The cheering section you visualized earlier. Just remember: in order to keep nutritious people in our lives, those relationships need to be mutually beneficial—you have to give as much, if not more, than you receive.

Toward the beginning of the chapter, you took the first step by outlining the people holding you back. Not only have you identified these individuals, but you mapped out what it is you will say to them to get them on board with you. If you want these people to remain in your lives, the dynamic of these relationships _must_ change. This may be scary, it may be uncomfortable, but it MUST be done. And you have to realize that part of creating the life you desire entails focusing on the good and letting go of the bad—be it bad influences, bad people, or bad situations.

Our next step was to identify the people you should surround yourself with. Some of these people are already in your life. Some relationships you will need to seek out. Spend time with these people (slot them into your "ideal schedule" and spend time cultivating these relationships). Thank them for supporting you. Ask them what successful qualities they see in you and how you might expand on those qualities. Seek out a mentor—someone who could be a *new* champion for you. Look at the list of people you want in your life and reach out to them. By overcoming your fear of letting go of the toxic relationships in your life, you will also be making room for the positive, encouraging people who want to see you succeed.

There are no excuses. You are now equipped with the knowledge of exactly who is holding you back, and you have outlined steps to get them out of your way. You also know the people already in your life and the people you want in your life to help you take it to the next level. What you do with this knowledge is up to you. But if you want to have a more fulfilled life and be the fabulous you I know you can be, you simply MUST take this critical step.

To drive the point home, let's review the steps needed to get there:

CHECKLIST

○ Outline the people who are holding you back and describe how these people make you feel when you are around them.

○ Develop a plan to either get these people on board with you ... or get them the heck off the bus!

○ List the nutritious people who are already in your life.

○ Make a list of the nutritious people or organizations you want to add to your life and outline your plan to reach them.

····· *Chapter 7* ·····

YOU TOO CAN TEACH YOUR SPOUSE TO ASK FOR DIRECTIONS

"I would say that the surest measure of a man's or a woman's maturity is the harmony, style, joy, and dignity he creates in his marriage, and the pleasure and inspiration he provides for his spouse."

— BENJAMIN SPOCK

NOW THAT WE HAVE DETERMINED WHO IS IN YOUR CHEERING SECTION, LET'S SPEND TIME DISCUSSING SOMEONE WHO SHOULD BE (OR SHOULD QUICKLY BECOME) ONE OF YOUR BIGGEST SUPPORTERS ... YOUR SPOUSE! For some of you, you may be going through this grand adventure as a single mom ... and kudos to you. I know it's a tough job! If that is the case for you, you can skip right over this chapter—or read it so you'll have some nice nuggets of info to share with all your married girlfriends.

For the rest of us, let's dig in and talk a bit about the other child taking up residence in our homes ... our spouse! If your brood is anything like mine, your partner often acts like one more child you are responsible for cleaning up after and dressing, and making sure he eats right! So much for that 50/50 partnership we signed up for when we said "I do." Now, I will say that after more than a decade of marriage, Shaun has come a long way (he can now dress himself ... as long as he's not going to be around anyone I know ... then, I still insist on picking out a matching outfit!). He cooks, cleans (well, *his* version of clean), and shares equally, if not more, in the household duties. How did we get here? you ask. How was it that I managed to train one of those "male creatures" and mold him into an equal participant around the house? These, my friends, are the tips (and tricks) I am going to share with you throughout this chapter.

Let me start by ensuring that we are all on the same page in terms of the division of duties within the house. Personally, I have a *very* strong bias that times have changed and gone are the days of women completing all of the household duties while the menfolk sit around in their business suits watching television and waiting for dinner to be served (a la *Leave It to Beaver*)! That may have worked fine in the days when the women did not work full-time jobs and when we did not contribute financially to the household. But the last time I checked, we working moms weren't exactly sitting around the house eating bonbons! As partners in the working portion of our household, we should (and must) expect to have partners in terms of the household duties. If you disagree with me on this point, I really don't know what to say. If you aren't willing to get your hubby (and kids, for that matter) to step up to the plate and help you out around the house, then don't expect to have much time for anything else besides work, cooking, and cleaning … and realize that by doing this, you completely relinquish the right to bitch and complain about all the work you have to do around the house!

If you are one who agrees with me, and refuses to shoulder the entire burden of household duties, let's talk about some of the ways to effectively divide the duties. Everything does not need to be divided equally, but every member of the household (who is old enough) should contribute to the running of and maintenance of the home. This is really quite easy to tackle (when you have a willing partner). It starts by talking with your spouse (and kids) about splitting up some of the chores. If you meet some resistance here, your discussion should go something like this:

To your spouse:

"I have really been working a lot on my own personal growth and on making sure I am a much happier and more fulfilled person—which will make me a better spouse to you and a better mom to the kids. One of the things I could really use help with is figuring out a way to divide up some of the things that need

to be done around the house. Let's look at a list of all the stuff we have to do around here and figure out who would be the best person to get it done. With all these things out of the way each day and week, we'll have more time to do fun stuff as a family (or with just the two of us!)."

See how we've used a couple of tools that soften the blow for our spouses. First, we pointed out that this will make us a better spouse … which benefits them. In his eyes … hubby doing housework equals happier wife … happier wife equals happier everyone! Second, we have asked for his help in figuring out how to do this. This is a very small version of the damsel-in-distress syndrome, where the men come in to rescue us. Now, you and I know we are in no way damsels in distress, but if we let the boys feel they are helping us problem-solve and fix this dilemma of ours … and it results in housework and cooking being done by someone other than us … I say play that card and play it fast!

Lastly, we go through the to-do list with our significant other so that we can determine who is best suited for the duties … and for the simple fact that they will then have no right to complain about a chore *they* chose for themselves! Creative, aren't we?! Now, you are all astute ladies, so I feel certain that you have incorporated some (if not all) of these little tricks to get your way before … so why not try it out on something worthwhile and with a more lasting effect? In all seriousness, though, this is the way to communicate with your spouse in *all* matters: state your thoughts and ask for the help you need. Then brainstorm the solution—together.

Let's put our plan to work and outline the things that need to get done around the house. We'll start you off with a list of common chores—and you add in others unique to your family.

Cooking	Taking out the Garbage
Sweeping / Mopping	Getting the Mail
Cleaning the Bathrooms	Paying the Bills
Packing the Kids' Lunches	Family Shuttle Service
Vacuuming	_____
Dusting	_____
Yardwork	_____
Cleaning the Kitchen	_____
Doing the Dishes	_____
Laundry	_____
Making the Beds	_____
Cleaning the Kids' Rooms	_____

Now that you have outlined things that need to get done, here comes the fun part. Finding people … other than just you … to get them done! If you have been fortunate enough to have a spouse and children who help out, congrats! You should use this as an opportunity to make sure the sweat equity of each member of the team is somewhat equal and fitting to everyone's interests and strengths. For the rest of you, use this as an exercise not only in delegation but also in fostering teamwork and a sense of purpose in regard to your household.

Despite the fact that many people absolutely abhor doing chores, there is actually some satisfaction to be found if you delegate properly. For example, I had a business associate whose husband was the police chief for a very large metropolitan area. As you would assume, his was an extremely stressful and difficult job. His wife shared with me that one of the things that tended to relieve his stress and relax him when he had a particularly difficult day was vacuuming! He loved it! So, this became one of his chores (and one less thing she had to do around the house). In fact, he loved it so much that, for a present one year, she had a central vac installed, just for him!

Be creative in filling in your chore list … think of things you would really like to do or that you have a particular propensity for. One of the easiest tasks to delegate should be *cooking* (although a lot of families share in this responsibility as their travel or work schedules dictate). However, if you are fortunate enough to have a spouse (or a teenager) who loves to cook and is good at it, this should be the first thing on his or her list. I am pretty fortunate in this regard. Shaun is a great cook—which comes in handy since I don't really "cook" as much as "fix" meals. I can "fix" a bowl of cereal or some microwave pancakes. I can "fix" a pot of noodles and open a jar of sauce. But aside from these very simple tasks, I am rather limited. I do appear to have a modicum of intelligence, so I can manage to follow clearly outlined recipes. Besides, my skill set is elsewhere … I can vacuum like crazy and make the meanest bed you've seen!

The key is to divide the list so that no one is miserable with his or her responsibilities (aside from cleaning the bathrooms … you may have to rock-paper-scissors for that one!). It's also imperative to realize there is absolutely nothing wrong with taking shortcuts now and then. As working moms who sometimes squeeze in seventy hours of work a week, we need shortcuts to help us keep our sanity. Here are a few I have found to be particularly helpful (I am hereby giving you permission to use them … despite what your mom or grandma may tell you!):

- Instant mac and cheese is an absolutely fine meal (not everything needs to be a home-cooked five-course extravaganza).
- Takeout is a great end to a very busy day (plus, you can buy one of those cute little boxes to keep all the menus in!).
- Most grocery stores feature fully prepared gourmet meals (by law we have to provide our children with food … I don't think it says we actually have to be the one to cook it!).
- You've GOT TO find a local business or grocery store that sells fresh prepared gourmet meals you can take home and freeze for later. All you have to do is freeze them until you're ready and pop 'em in the oven (or on the stove, depending on the dish).
- There is absolutely nothing wrong with a housekeeper or maid service (even if only once every few weeks for the deep cleaning that takes so much of our time).
- Things don't have to be perfect (we'll talk about this in more detail in the "If It Ain't Broke, Don't Fix It" chapter). If the kids' rooms are less than perfect, that's OK … that's what doors were

made for! If they have soda twice during a week, they'll survive. Let's face it: when we die, our gravestone is not going to say "Here lies Kristin … a devoted mother, despite the fact her children's rooms were only *partially* clean and overlooking the cavity her oldest had at age 9!" We've got to be OK with the fact that life isn't perfect! This one I definitely preach quite a bit better than I practice, but, hey, I'm working on it!

- The fifteen-year-old boy down the street will cut the grass cheap (certainly for much less than what YOU make in an hour)!
- Grocery stores deliver! Just think of all the money you will save without your toddler hanging on your leg in the ice cream aisle screaming "Please, Mommy, please!" and your teenager throwing item after item into your cart. You'll save time AND $$$. Wooooo hooooo!

The key with taking shortcuts is they should save you time and energy. You need to look at the overall picture. What is best for you and your family as a whole? What will go further in creating the life you want—a life full of joy, excitement, and fulfillment? Is your time better spent deep-cleaning toilets on a Saturday afternoon or taking the kids to a park or out for ice cream? What could you outsource to free up more time for your family? In each of the chores and responsibilities you will assign in the next exercise, I want you to think about getting them done effectively and efficiently so that you have more time for the things that are really important: you, your spouse, your kids, your family, your friends, your career, and your community—the same seven categories we worked to make time for back in Chapter 5.

Keeping our priorities in mind, let's fill in the "Household Responsibility Chart." As you do, remember, no one ever cried out from her deathbed: "I wish I had spent more time making the bed." Start by taking the to-do items from the list you created earlier in this chapter and assign them to someone—and that someone does NOT need to always be YOU! The rules are simple:

- Every chore needs to be assigned.
- Chores CAN be shared by multiple people.
- If you have more than one child, indicate who is responsible for the items on their list.

- Hired help and shortcuts don't have to be incorporated daily or even weekly. But they DO need to be incorporated. Just list the ones you think will come in handy on those days when you're about to "lose it"!

Household Responsibility Chart

Mom	Dad	Kids	Hired Help	Shortcuts

Now that the major things are out of the way, I want to put your minds at ease a bit. There are some things that you probably didn't list above that are unique to your family and that you simply MUST retain control over. And, once again, I am here to give you *permission* to do just that … retain control.

Let me give you a couple of small examples. In my house, it is an absolute must that I pack all suitcases for every member of our family whenever we go on a trip. Sure, Shaun is physically capable of taking clothes from the closets and moving them gingerly into suitcases, but he lacks quite a bit in the preparation department. As most moms do, for each family vacation, I carefully figure out how long we will be gone (critical when determining how many pairs of underwear to pack), what events we have planned (you can't wear a swimsuit to a fancy dinner), and the toiletries and other items that will be needed (nine days without my make-up would be enough to scare the children!). I then lay out all of the items to ensure we have everything, and into the suitcase they go. Voila! We're on our way, with everything we need (and then some) in tow.

The other area I used to have trouble delegating (and chose to hold onto as often as my schedule allowed) was the children's doctor visits. When emergencies arose, I was completely comfortable with either of us taking the kids to the doc. And, believe me, we had our share (I think they may have named a wing of the peds ER after Bailey!). What I had trouble delegating was the routine checkups. I don't know if any of you have tried this, ladies; but as a general rule, husbands suck at dealing with routine medical exams. To further explain my insistence on taking the girls in for their routine visits, I have to go back to one of Bailey's early well visits. She was less than a couple of years old and was still in the stage of getting a number of vaccinations each time she went in for a checkup. For one such visit, I was unable to make the appointment (the first and last time), so Shaun happily agreed to take her. I instructed Shaun to call me after the appointment to let me know how it went (as any good mom would do). And Shaun, being the well-trained spouse that he is, promptly called as soon as he returned to the car. The conversation went something like this:

Me: *"How did the appointment go?"*

Shaun: *"Fine."*

Me: *"Did the doctor say anything I need to know?"*

Shaun: *"No."*

Me: *"Was there anything we should be concerned with?"*

Shaun: *"He didn't mention anything."*

Me: *"Is there anything we should be doing that we're not?"* (I wanted to ensure we were hitting all the developmental milestones, of course).

Shaun: *"I didn't ask."*

NOW, HERE'S WHERE THE STORY GETS GOOD ...

Me: *"Did she get any shots?"*

Shaun: *"Yeah. A bunch of them. They had one extra one that
          wasn't required. They said it was an optional vaccine. It
          wasn't covered by insurance, but it was only like 50 bucks,
          so I told 'em to go ahead."*

Me: *"What was the vaccine for?"*

Shaun: *"I think it was for* **scurvy***!"*

Are you kidding me ... scurvy?! We aren't living in a third-world
country, and last I checked my child had not just come over on the
Mayflower. But my dear husband thought it appropriate to immunize our
infant for a disease that she had no chance of actually contracting! As it
turns out, the vaccine was, in fact, NOT for scurvy (although the nurse at
the doctor's office found my story quite amusing when I called to find out
definitively what shot had actually been given to Bailey). So, Shaun's days
of taking the children to their physician checkups started and ended in
that one day!

I must warn you girls: sometimes the men in our lives try to trick
us with things like this. Some years later, I learned that Shaun *knew* the
vaccine was NOT for scurvy (although he really had no idea what it
actually *was* for). He said he knew that by telling me that he had Bailey
immunized for scurvy, he would promptly be fired from doctor-visit
duty! That sneaky S.O.B. (I thought only us girls played tricks like that).
So the moral is: don't leave any room for error. After his admission, he
was promptly returned to doctor duty (although he now goes to the
physician equipped with a detailed list of appropriate questions, which I
carefully write out the night before the appointment). We both got a good
laugh out of the tricks we play to get out of doing the things we don't like
(or aren't equipped) to do. His other classic is loading the dishwasher
in the most idiotic way, so that three plates—all laid out flat—and one
pot and about six cups are all that fit ... a lame attempt at getting out

of doing the dishes! Again, this was quickly remedied with a "how to properly load the dishwasher" lesson. Dishes are now squarely under the "Shaun" column on the Andree "Household Responsibility Chart." That's what he gets for trying to trick me—right, ladies?

The point is, whatever your "thing" may be, whether it is packing the suitcases, taking the kids to the doctor, or folding the laundry—it is OK to hang onto those precious tasks yourself. After all, with some things, Mom really does know best!

OK. Now that we have rallied the troops and are well on our way to a clean house, manicured yard, and full tummy, and have figured out the tasks we just can't (or don't choose to) let go, let's talk about some other areas where we could use the support of our betrothed. I will begin with an area I constantly hear some of my girlfriends complaining about … and a number of my male co-workers commenting on … the topic of caring for one's own children.

Make no bones about it: this is an area where I have very little tolerance. In the spirit of full disclosure, I must say that I am and have always been very fortunate in this regard. Shaun plays more than an equal role in watching our children (although most of the disciplinary action still lands squarely on my shoulders). But in the stories I hear from others (and likely what I would hear from many of you), this is not the case. Some husbands simply refuse to watch their own children or just assume that YOU will always be there to supervise and "tend to" the young 'uns. This is absolutely bogus. We should not have to ASK our husbands if they are willing to "watch the kids" while we go to the grocery store or run out to get our nails done … they are their kids too! Unless you are some freak of nature or have given birth to the Second Coming, those little seedlings didn't magically implant themselves in your uterus! There was no Immaculate Conception, so my guess is that dear ol' hubby played his part. And, in doing so, signed himself up for daddy duty.

Nothing aggravates me more than to hear one of my male friends with young children *complain* that he has to "baby-sit the kids tonight." It is NOT baby-sitting when they are YOUR children. I am quite familiar with baby-sitting—it involves a teenager coming over to your house to watch your children in exchange for a sum of money (and a very high sum at that!). Nowhere in the definition of baby-sitting does it mention the word "father." And, I am assuming that you are not actually paying your husband for this duty. If you are, just stop reading right now and immediately give me a call … we've got some major one-on-one coaching to be done here!

It is their God-given duty to care for their children, which should occasionally involve watching the kiddos without you around. I know it may be frightening at first, but this HAS TO happen. Sure, you will likely come home to find that the kids had popcorn and Ho Hos for dinner, and that they went to bed without a bath and without brushing their teeth, but after a few "discussions" with the hubby on appropriate dinner and bedtime routines, things should begin to fall into place. And, I am assuming we aren't starting from square one here, where your husband has NEVER watched the children alone, so it shouldn't take too much effort to make this a standard part of your household routine. I promise it will pay off—especially financially. I can't tell you how much money we save when Shaun stays home with the kids so that I can do the grocery shopping or make a quick Target run (we save even more when Shaun does the shopping and I stay home … he can stick to a shopping list like nobody's business, where I spend $100 running into Target to pick up toilet paper and toothpaste!).

Bottom line: if your husband isn't pulling his weight in the child-care department, tell him to get off his lazy butt and contribute! If he expects you to watch the little darlings when he has an early tee time on Saturday morning, then he should OFFER to step up so that you can join the girls for a Friday night girls' night out (which we will talk more about in Chapter 13). Let's evaluate how we're doing.

Does my hubby regularly watch the kids (without my having to beg, plead, and offer up s-e-x?)

○ Yes   ○ No

If you answered "yes" to this, congrats and keep up the great (and equal) work. If your answer was "no," I want you to outline below the "discussion" you plan to have with your man, who also happens to be the sperm donor for your children. (I do realize that in some cases your spouse may not be the biological father of your children, BUT, unless you were hiding the fact that you had children from him until after he said "I do," he knew what he was getting into and you should fully EXPECT him to contribute in this area.)

Here's what I am gonna say … and I'm stickin' to my guns:

HONEY...

It seems like these are things we should not even have to mention. After all, getting your spouse to share in the family responsibilities is something everyone should be addressing, in every household across America. Yet, I do have to mention it—in fact, *I had to devote an entire chapter to it.* Why? Because of the countless stories we all hear from women who have completely *neglected* this in their lives. They are among the millions of working moms, like you, who are trying to be Superwoman and do everything themselves. They assume that the only way to get things done, and get them done right, is to do them themselves. Just as it will in your business life, this type of behavior will destroy your personal life. You have to be able to relinquish some of the things we have mentioned if you are to lead a fulfilled life. No one was put on this earth expected to handle everything all by herself. No one can. The key to being able to delegate effectively is that you must have a high degree of trust in the person to whom you are delegating. And if you can't trust your spouse, you have much greater issues than needing someone to help you around the house.

As simple as they are in concept and in execution, these critical things will go a long way in creating a more fulfilling life for yourself. A life in which you are no longer wasting time on trivial things and aren't constantly trying to "do it all" yourself. You will become more acutely aware of the time you spend on things that could easily be done by others. You will begin to look for and expect equality in your relationship, an equality that now stretches across your household and child-rearing duties. I can't even describe for you the difference these things have made in my life ... in our lives. I lead a much more blessed life ... a more fulfilled life, because I truly feel like we are *sharing* our lives and all the to-dos that come along with running a household and raising a family. I urge you to strive to do the same.

One of the keys in doing this is to have open lines of communication. Without this, it will be impossible to share in the household responsibilities, including disciplining the children. Good communication goes a long way in not always painting one parent as the "bad guy." In our house, I am definitely the strict one, but we work to communicate with each other and with the children to ensure we are all on the same page. Then it isn't just Mommy being the mean one. When I was growing up, it was not *at all* that way in my house. My mom was *clearly* the strict one (a.k.a. the "mean" one) who was always telling us what we could and couldn't do. She was the one who always said "no." And my dad was the "yes" guy.

They agreed, to a large extent, on the things they would and would not let us do, but the difference was in the execution. If there was something that they were going to let us do, such as go to the skating rink or to the mall, my dad would be the one to say "Of course you can go!" But if it was something they weren't planning on agreeing to, such as letting us stay out until midnight on a school night, my dad would simply say "Go ask your mother." He knew the answer was going to be "no," but instead of being the one to deliver that message, he let my mom be the bad guy! And Dad loved being the good guy. Now, I am a true daddy's girl to this very day; but c'mon, Dad ... that was sneaky! I didn't realize what was going on when I was a child, but as an adult I figured it all out ... and

I'll be darned if I'm gonna let that happen in my house! So, I strive extra hard to make sure we talk through things and present a united front on all decisions (besides, kids are pretty smart … it will take BOTH of you to outwit them!).

Further, open communication is key to ensure both partners are getting the support they need. It is impossible to know when one person is overwhelmed and when the other needs to step it up a bit, unless you can BOTH share what you are experiencing. If you can't talk to your spouse openly and honestly and share with him the things you want and need, you've got a bigger problem (and I would recommend you speak with a professional therapist to work through your communication issues and learn to have a healthy dialogue). However, if you make a conscious effort toward an open dialogue, you will find that you are creating a true *partnership*, which is critical in leading a full life.

Having the right people on your side and having your spouse engaged are key. Life is too difficult to walk alone. Now that you've taken steps to make sure you have people in the stands to cheer you on, you won't have to. But before we move on to the *things* that are holding you back, let's take a moment to recap this chapter's exercises.

CHECKLIST

○ Outline your family to-do list.

○ Make a list of shortcuts that will buy you some much-needed time.

○ Divvy up the duties by completing the "Household Responsibility Chart" (refer to the Appendix for a copy of this template for you to display for your housemates to see!).

○ Decide on the things YOU will keep control of (so you don't have a stroke worrying if the dear man you married will ever do it right!). Don't become frustrated with the things he just can't do ... perhaps it isn't in his makeup! Just as changing a tire may not be in yours ... hey, another shortcut idea ... join the AAA motor club ... it works for flat tires and lost keys!

○ This is an ongoing one ... ensure that the lines of communication between you and your spouse ALWAYS remain open.

····· Chapter 8 ·····

TIME FOR A TUNE-UP

"Challenges are what make life interesting;
overcoming them is what makes life meaningful."

— JOSHUA J. MARINE

IN CHAPTER 6, WE UNCOVERED THE PEOPLE HOLDING YOU BACK. Now we are going to spend some time uncovering and putting an end to the *things* holding you back from living the life you desire. In my own life and in my work with other professional women, I have found some common trends that seem to pop up over and over again relating to the *things* that hold people back. And we're going to tackle them one by one.

It may be hard to admit that we fall victim to some of these things. After all, when you take a closer look, a number of them just seem ridiculous. But only by admitting that they are issues in our lives can we implement strategies to overcome them. As someone who has probably had each of these things hold me back at one time or another in my life, I can attest to the fact that the sooner you realize you are falling victim and take the necessary steps to change your behavior, the faster you will be on a path toward to a more fulfilled life.

As I see it, here are the common mistakes that many women make that stop us dead in our tracks and keep us living the same ol' same ol' every day: 1.) Exaggerating your problems, 2.) Lack of focus, 3.) The habits you build, 4.) Fear of failure, 5.) Fear of success, 6.) Fear of taking risks, and 7.) Procrastination.

Let's start off with a little reality check. I want you to make a "✓" by all of the items you feel are holding you back in certain areas of your life, be they personal or professional:

○ Exaggerating your problems (stressing over things that really aren't that important)
○ Lack of focus (losing sight of the big picture)
○ The habits you build (good habits AND bad ones)
○ Fear of failure (so scared you'll fail that it holds you back)
○ Fear of success (holding back because you're not sure you can handle all that comes along with it)
○ Fear of taking risks (too fearful to even get started)
○ Procrastination (we'll talk about this one later— ha-ha!)

And, just like the *Cosmo* quiz, let's rate how you did:

0-2 ✓'s

Ladies, ladies … congratulations! Either you have already learned worthwhile strategies to keep these things from acting as roadblocks on your way to a successful life or … you are lying through your teeth! If you are one of the fortunate ones who do not employ any of these success stoppers, I would expect you to already be living the life you desire … or at least on a solid path to get there. If not, look at the list again and really think about it. Or, better yet, ask your accountability partner to check off the ones she or he sees you falling victim to.

But seriously, for the three of you who can seriously say that only one or two of these items are holding you back—honey, you're well on your way! But keep reading—you can share the tips with your less-put-together girlfriends.

3-5 ✓'s

This is more along the line of where I see most accomplished women falling. Perhaps you are a risk taker when it comes to certain things, such as making a career change, but once you do, have a fear of failure so strong that it stifles you. Or maybe you have laser-sharp focus but have become a pro at exaggerating all the problems that seem to creep up in your life … all the reason why you aren't accomplishing what you set out to.

Bottom line is this: you are just like the 95 percent of other women out there who do an incredible job at a lot of things in their lives but have a few things still holding them back. In the sections that follow, I will give you some strategies to overcome the areas holding you back. Pay particular attention to the categories you outlined as being problematic for you. But don't forget to give the other categories a good read too— that way you will know how to tackle them should they ever become an issue (or should a friend need your guidance in that area).

6-7 ✓'s

To quote the kids … OMG! We have definitely got some work to do here. Let me be frank. First, you are not alone. There are thousands of other moms out there who have problems in a lot of these areas. Trust me, I used to be one of them! I excelled at exaggerating all of the terrible things that were going to happen to me (most of which never actually happened!). I was scared of failing yet wasn't quite sure how to deal with success either. I shied away from taking too big a risk in most areas of my life. And I was the queen of procrastination—while I always got everything done by the deadline and got it done well, I waited until the eleventh hour to actually start doing things. Sound familiar?

Second, you can overcome these roadblocks. There are strategies we will put in place to move these boulders right out of your path and allow you to have a clean shot at creating the life you desire.

With all of these areas to tackle, we better get moving (we wouldn't want to procrastinate now, would we?).

Exaggerating your problems

This one is such a huge issue for a number of women that we're going to devote an entire chapter to it later in the book. But for now, let's talk about how some of us gals have a tendency to blow things out of proportion.

Let me be among the first to tell you, most things that "happen" to you aren't that big a flippin' deal. Just as I mentioned earlier in the book when describing my former associate, stuff happens—our baby sitters get sick, our cars crap out ... heck, we moms even feel under the weather sometimes (I still haven't figured how to keep the house neat and clean during that one), but the truth of the matter is that it doesn't kill us. It usually doesn't even slow us down for more than a little bit. Yet I see mom after mom allowing this to hold them back.

Picture this. One of your best girlfriends (also a Type A mom) calls you between two of the fifteen meetings you have scheduled for the day. She launches into a twenty-minute dissertation about how the idiot behind her in traffic this morning rammed into the back of her SUV and it took half an hour for the cops to get there to file a report. By that point, she was late to drop off Ashton and Ian at the sitter and was then late to a big meeting she had. Next she tells you how that wreck will probably cost her the big promotion she has been waiting for—after all, why would she be promoted after coming in late for a meeting. And if she doesn't get the promotion, she won't be able to get the new house. And without the new house, her family won't be able to move into that better school district she was telling you about. And ... And ... And...

Are you getting the picture? How many of you have been on the receiving end of these conversations? Worse yet, how many of you have been the instigator? In the spirit of complete and utter honesty here, I have to tell you that I was the master of these doom-and-gloom scenarios. From the time I was in middle school, I managed to find a way to link getting a B in social studies to having to work cleaning out sewers for the rest of my life. It wasn't until I learned to take a minute to relax and to look at the whole situation that I was finally able to rid myself of this nasty habit. It still rears its ugly head every now and then, especially when I am particularly stressed, but I now recognize what I'm doing.

I want you to think about a time recently when you exaggerated your problems (describe ... and don't forget to include all the stupid, unrealistic things you just knew were going to happen as a result):

_____

_____

_____

How did this make you feel?

_____

My guess is that not only did it drain all your energy in that moment, but it also made you less secure about the future. So why in the heck do we do things like this? As busy moms, we have a zillion things going through our heads at one time—deadlines at work, school projects, bus and field trip schedules, birthdays, shopping lists, and on and on and on and on. It's no wonder that when something comes into play that throws us off our game, it gets us all out of whack! The challenge is NOT to keep these things from happening. It's impossible—the unexpected is a part of life (without which imagine how bored we'd be!). The challenge is to learn to recognize that a flat tire will not lead to your getting fired. Forgetting to give your kids lunch money will not mean they die of starvation (the school will actually feed them ... believe me, I've done it on more than one occasion).

Look back over how you felt the last time you made a mountain out of a molehill (as Mom used to say). There's no time for that in our busy lives. You have to make a choice—and make it now—that you will not fall victim to this trap. You'll slip from time to time (just as I do), and that's OK ... but as soon as you realize what you are doing, you have to STOP IT ... right then! Just as you would say to your child, "You stop that this instant!" Only then will you reclaim control over your life and control over this little thing that's holding you back!

I heard a quote (not sure who said it, but I absolutely love it): "My life is full of catastrophes, most of which have never happened." Just as in our lives, most of the "catastrophes" we fear have little chance of actually happening. To continue moving toward a fulfilled life, you have to MAKE SURE you are not making the problems that do come any bigger than they are. Deal with it … and move on!

Here is how we are going to attack this issue: For the next several weeks (or longer if you're a slow learner), ask your accountability partner to give you a little slap (figuratively, of course) every time you start to exaggerate your problems. Make your partner point them out to you every time he or she sees you doing this. After a few "smacks," you should be able to pick up on the trend and start to catch *yourself* before you waste any more valuable time.

Here's a to-do item for you: I want each of you to go out and *get yourself a journal* so you can capture the times you "exaggerate your problems," as well as to journal about the other areas in this chapter that affect your life. Keep a list of the things you blow out of proportion. Not only should you list the "thing" itself, but you should also describe what you fear the ultimate disposition of the problem will be—i.e., the "terrible thing" you just know will happen. Then list what ultimately DID happen. What you are bound to see is that most often the ultimate disposition of our problems is nowhere near what we constructed in our minds. Once you begin to recognize this pattern, it becomes easier for you to see what a complete and utter waste it is to use our valuable time and energy on things so stupid! Keep your journal nearby until you have control over this area in your life. Share your journal entries with your accountability partner. Once you actually verbalize them to someone else, once you say OUT LOUD the ridiculous things you have fabricated in your mind, you will *easily* see how much a time and energy zapper they really are! And how they are keeping you from leading a life of joy and fulfillment. You fix this piece of this puzzle, and you are well on your way.

Lack of focus

Focus (or lack thereof) is another area where I see many of my female counterparts beginning to lose control. And why shouldn't they? With the umpteen things on our to-do list, it's no wonder our minds tend to wander from thing to thing and task to task. What I am referring to here is less a matter of changing the task we are focusing on, but rather the fact that frequently women have a tendency to either lose focus or to focus on the wrong thing.

Let's start with losing focus. HUGE problem here, ladies … HUGE. It is in the moments when we lose focus that self-doubt and fear creep in. So it's not just the loss of focus but the compounded effect that doubt and fear play on our minds and our actions (or inactions). Too often, we are so tuned in to the little things on our list that we take our eyes off the ball. We lose focus on the big picture. And it is the big picture—our overriding goal—that motivates us.

Too often I see people focus on all the wrong things—on things that have no relevance whatsoever to the goals they are trying to achieve. Keep your big goal in mind and do the things you must to achieve that goal—make sure that your actions, ALL your actions, align with achieving that goal. Focus involves not only what you do but more importantly what you DON'T do. One surefire way to NOT achieve your goal is to waste valuable time on things that have no relevance whatsoever to hitting your goal. As John Carmack put it, "Focus is a matter of deciding what things you're not going to do."

If your goal is to be a world-class athlete, you're NOT going to go out every night with your friends and you ARE going to get plenty of rest so that you are in top shape for that 6 a.m. practice. Likewise, if your goal is to land a huge account at your ad firm, you ARE going to spend your time developing and providing the client with ingenious ideas and outlining the positive effect these ideas will have on the client's bottom line. You are NOT going to spend your time on subpar ideas or on mulling over all the obstacles that stand in your way. Strive to focus 90 percent of your time on solutions and only 10 percent of your time on the problems you face. Too often I see women spending time obsessing about the things going wrong instead of putting effort toward creating solutions. This, ladies, is typical avoidance behavior—and it will get you absolutely nowhere!

When was the last time you made these mistakes? When you either completely lost focus or focused too long on the problem rather than the solution?

_____

_____

_____

Think of the time and energy you wasted on this lack of (proper) focus. If you find yourself falling victim to this limiting behavior, here is the remedy. For each project or overriding goal you are working on, develop a goal sheet. You don't need to write a novel; so if you have fifty goals on your annual plan, break it down a bit further. Take one current project (or goal) you are working on and write that goal at the top of your sheet. Next, make a list of the items/steps you need to focus on to bring you closer to realizing that goal. Last, list the things you find yourself focusing on that have absolutely nothing (or very little) to do with reaching your goal. Keep this list on your desk or in your planner—somewhere you will see it often. Not only will this frequently remind you of your goal, but it will also serve as a check-in as to whether you're keeping your focus on what's important. Do this for any other big goals you have or projects you are working on.

Here's a sample to get you started.

GOAL:
Bring in ten new clients in the next quarter.

FOCUS ITEMS:

○ Daily calls to centers of influence and current clients with the purpose of prospecting.
○ Attend networking functions—at least one per week.
○ Update my social networking profiles to ensure I am maximizing their potential (and set a goal with each of those sites).

THINGS THAT GET ME OFF-TRACK:
○ I get caught up in paperwork—I need to make sure I am delegating all nonessential paperwork to my assistant.
○ I spend time answering e-mails instead of getting on the phone.
○ I spend too much time socializing at networking functions and forget to go into them with a goal of meeting five interesting people in my target market whom I will follow up with.

Now, let's create your own list:

GOAL:

_____

_____

_____

FOCUS ITEMS:

○ _____

○ _____

○ _____

○ _____

○ _____

THINGS THAT GET ME OFF-TRACK:

○ _____

○ _____

○ _____

○ _____

○ _____

Let's recap: First, we're going to stop exaggerating our problems. This goes for at home as well as at the office. No more "I am definitely getting fired for this one" and no more "I swear, I've gained so much weight, I weigh 500 pounds" (unless of course you DO weigh 500 pounds; in that case, honey, get yourself to a doctor … now!).

Next, we are going to focus our energies and our efforts on the task at hand—and quit spending our valuable resources where they don't belong! Quit *talking* about doing the things you need to do and actually *do* them. Talk is cheap … and I don't know about you, but I'm no cheap mama!

In doing both of these things, we are going to use our journal to document when we "fall off the wagon." Now let's move on to roadblock No. 3.

The habits you build

Let's spend some time talking about the habits we build. In terms of habits, it's pretty simple. Each of us, through our actions or inactions, builds habits. The successful career woman builds the habit of daily check-ins with her employees to ensure they are happy and productive. The unsuccessful woman builds the habit of ignoring the needs and musings of her employees. The successful mom builds the habit of asking her kids "How was school today?" and listens as they recount the day's triumphs and tragedies. The unsuccessful mom builds the habit of forgetting to even ask!

In a talk titled *The Common Denominator of Success*, first delivered in 1940 to a group of life insurance professionals, Albert E.N. Gray laid out what he found to be the common thread in all successful individuals. A simple fact that, with utmost certainty, can guide us all toward success. Gray states:

> *The common denominator of success—the secret of success of every man who has ever been successful—lies in the fact that he* ***formed the habit of doing things that failures don't like to do.***
> *It's just as true as it sounds and it's just as simple as it seems. You can hold it up to the light, you can put it to the acid test, and you can kick it around until it's worn out, but when you are all through with it, it will still be the common denominator of success, whether you like it or not.*

The point is this: we are ALL building habits—all the time. And we can build good habits or bad ones. Yet we must, at all times, ensure we are building the habits we need to build to be successful—that we are habitually doing the things unsuccessful people are unwilling to do!

The beautiful thing is that the types of habits we build are entirely up to us. What kinds of habits are you building? Are you doing the things you need to do to be a success in your career—or are you constantly putting things off? Do you gravitate toward doing the easy things and overlook the tougher but necessary tasks? Do you focus on the insignificant many vs. the critical few?

Only YOU know the habits you need to build. Habits shouldn't be judged by others. They should relate to helping you attain the specific goals and vision you have for your life. Let's take a look at how you're doing:

MY HABITS

Here are the good ones (to-do lists, prompt follow-through, etc.):

* _____
* _____
* _____
* _____
* _____

And here are the bad (procrastination, avoidance behaviors, not meeting deadlines):

* _____
* _____
* _____
* _____
* _____

Now, go back to the habits you listed above. Next to each of them write what you are going to do to ensure you continue the good ones (once you've been doing them awhile, this should come pretty easy). Next, take each of the bad habits and write what you plan to do to stop doing them or to turn them into good habits. For example, if you have gotten into the habit of putting off that mountain of awful (but necessary) paperwork until you have ten minutes left in the day, what are you going to do to tackle the problem earlier? If you have a goal of bringing in ten new clients this quarter, what are the precise steps you are going to take to get there?

As for how you are going to actually stick to your plan of continuing the good and stopping the bad, I have an idea for you! In my early years in the business, my performance coach gave me a little motivation that quickly turned my bad habits right around. She had me put a kicker on each of the daily goals I set. And this kicker, in all its simplicity, had a profound effect on my building good habits and squashing bad ones. What it entails is simple: you set a small goal, whether it is a daily goal or a two-week goal. Something that is a bite-sized piece and that will contribute to the attainment of a larger goal (such as the item you listed when you outlined a goal under the "focus" section). Once you do that, you attach the kicker, which can either be a reward or a consequence (depending on how you are motivated). If you hit your goal … thus building good habits … you get the reward! Likewise, if you don't hit your goal, you suffer the consequence!

One of the best examples of how this worked for me was in regard to my need to get referrals for my practice. Early in my career, I was working hard to build up my practice; and since I worked on a referral-only basis, it necessitated that I ask for referrals … a lot! I needed to ask everyone I met to introduce me to someone new. Simple in concept, but tough sometimes in execution. And, to compound the matter, I had built the habit of "forgetting" to ask for referrals (part bad habit, part avoidance behavior, but nonetheless I was in a rut!). I needed to break free of this bad habit and build a good one. So my business coach made me put some teeth into every goal I set. We would change the kicker from reward to consequence with each new goal, depending on how I felt motivated at that time. Perhaps the best one we ever used involved a consequence … a BIG one. To give you a little background, I have a severe and unhealthy addiction to Diet Coke (I know, I know, the aspartame is horrible for you … I am trying to break the habit … but for now, know that I am working on it!). Despite my unhealthy habit, the addiction proved to be a great motivator. I set a goal of getting twenty-five referrals one particular week; the kicker was that if I failed and did not get the twenty-five referrals, I had to lay off Diet Coke for an entire week. It may sound trivial, but I tell you … I never worked so hard to get referrals in my life (except perhaps when the *reward* for my twenty-five referrals was an order of McDonald's fries!). What's more … I hit my goal!

How can we apply this to you? Are you someone who is late to every meeting? If so, treat yourself to a new pair of shoes when you make it a week without being late for a single thing! Do you avoid making cold calls? Schedule phoning time early in the morning and then buy yourself and a girlfriend coffee to celebrate your success on the phone. Do you hit the snooze button ten times and still manage to oversleep? Commit to hitting it only once—and if you don't do that for an entire week, you have to get up an hour earlier the following week to make a nice breakfast for the entire family!

Building habits … *good habits* … is tough. It takes work. You have probably read the research that states it takes twenty-one days to build a habit. So, why not have some fun during those twenty-one days. Build in a reward to keep you moving in the right direction—to make those baby steps toward your goal a little bit more exciting. Look back to the items you listed in the last section as "Focus Items" and assign a reward or a consequence to them. Let your accountability partner in on this and ask him or her to hold you to it. Write about times you aren't building good habits in your journal—outline the things that seem to get you off-track … and how you plan to overcome them. Before long, you will have built solid habits, which will catapult you toward your goal.

That is, if we can keep *fear* from sidelining you …

Fear of failure

We are all busy working moms. We have a lot of balls in the air. We want a lot out of life, so we set big goals. Yet sometimes the very things we are striving for actually scare the crap out of us! We set a huge goal, think of all the wonderful things that will happen when we achieve it, and are raring to go. Then, all of a sudden, we start to think … and we get a little scared. A little fear is good—it keeps us moving forward, keeps us on our toes. But too much fear can stifle us and actually cause us to fail.

In order to keep fear from holding us back, we need to get in tune with the fact that some degree of failure WILL exist in each of our lives. And that it is in no way a bad thing. Failure is a necessity if we want to accomplish anything. If someone has never failed at anything, he or she is either a freak of nature or someone who has never accomplished anything! We all fail. We all fail a lot! If we didn't, how would we learn anything? Henry Ford (who we could go out on a limb and say accomplished a thing or two in his lifetime) said that "failure is the opportunity to begin again, more intelligently." I know what you're thinking—here she goes again with the quotes—but really, these people are good, and we should listen to them!

If you are a smart woman (which I know you are), you will learn from your mistakes. And the moment you realize that each failure brings you closer to success, you will have achieved a lot. You will have put yourself into a frame of mind whereby your fears of failure vanish … and you can "begin again more intelligently." The key is to not be afraid. Go into each opportunity without fear of failure.

What are the things you aren't trying, personally and professionally, because you are afraid of failing?:

- _____
- _____
- _____
- _____
- _____

Be honest with yourself. What is the worst that could happen if you attempted these things and weren't successful? With most things, failure won't make you go flat broke, won't kill you, and likely won't get you fired. Why then are we so afraid to attempt new things? Why do YOU have a fear of failure—and why are YOU letting that fear keep you from trying and accomplishing great things?

> Describe exactly what you are afraid of here:
>
> _____
>
> _____
>
> _____
>
> _____

Most people who indicate "fear of failure" as one of the areas they struggle with are FAR underutilizing their gifts and completely underestimating the incredible things they can accomplish in their lives. Imagine what your life would be like if you went after what you wanted, without fear of failing. Look at the list above of things you aren't trying because you're afraid you might fail. What would your life look like if you went out and actually accomplished each of them?

Here's another quote for you, a spin on a famous Babe Ruth quote from the movie *A Cinderella Story* starring Hilary Duff (let go of your fear, ladies, and admit that you too have seen this teenage comedy ... great story line ... brought tears to my eyes!). In the movie, a quote written on the wall of the diner that Hilary's father owned read: "*Never let the fear of striking out keep you from playing the game.*" What a great but simple truth. It's as if everything we need to know in life we can learn from teenage TV shows and movies! Scary, isn't it?

But really ... what is fear and why do we so frequently let it stand in our way? Perhaps you have heard that FEAR stands for **F**alse **E**vidence **A**ppearing **R**eal. Therein lies the key ... it is FALSE evidence we perceive to be real. There is no truth to it. There is no absolute that if we attempt what we are afraid of that we are going to fail. It's not rational ... it's made up ... we imagined it to justify staying in the same comfortable place where we've always existed.

Ladies, if you want to change your life, you have to change the way you act. You have to recognize when fear is holding you back. Then you have to take it a step further and address those fears. Never make a decision not to attempt something based on fear. It is like Eleanor Roosevelt said: "You must do the thing you think you cannot do." Only by doing that which you fear will you be able to conquer any unreasonable fear of failure. But that is not all there is to it. To expand, let me share with you more of Mrs. Roosevelt's quote (the part that is typically omitted): "You gain strength, courage and confidence in every experience in which you really stop to look fear in the face. ... You must do the thing you think you cannot do." By looking fear in the face and going into those fears, we gain a courage and a confidence that we cannot gain otherwise. Not only do we allow ourselves the chance to succeed at the task at hand, but we also create within ourselves an "I can do it" attitude, which permeates into other decisions and other areas of our lives. Each and every time you look fear in the face and keep moving forward, you are working to create that "tough little cookie" we know it takes to juggle all the ups and downs and trials and triumphs working moms have to contend with every day. We don't have time to fear failure ... hell, we don't have time to do anything other than the tasks at hand ... we're MOMS! And the less time we spend in moments of fear and weakness, the more time we have for the things that really matter in our lives!

When you find yourself falling victim to the fear of failure, use your journal and capture those moments. Describe your fear—outline and clearly define what you are afraid of. Then go out and do the thing you fear. Look the task right in the face and go after it. Next, write how you felt when you did so. Regardless if you succeeded or failed at the task, describe how you felt for having *attempted* the feat. Throughout your lifetime, you will win some and lose some—and that is not the issue. The issue is: in order to win, you have to be in the game. And you can't do that if you won't even walk onto the field. To be a strong, empowered woman, in your personal life AND your professional one, you have to be willing to put yourself out there—and to "not let the fear of failure keep you from playing the game." Not only will you lead a life rich with adventures and accomplishments, but you will be setting an amazing example for your children.

Now, let's tackle another type of fear ...

Fear of success

As crazy as it sounds, many women (and men too, for that matter) actually fear success. They set lofty goals, dream big things, and just when they are well on their way to hitting those goals, they stop short! It's as if they are scared to take those last few steps. Scared to realize the dream they claim to have been longing for.

I see this play out with a lot of professionals, and it appears to the outside observer that they are actually trying to sabotage their own efforts. It's crazy, right? We set a goal, work hard to achieve it , and then stop short! I have a friend who works in the financial services industry who is on the verge of some really great accomplishments—truthfully, she is teetering on the edge of reaching the top 5 percent of our industry … worldwide! A huge accomplishment. She has been on the verge of this each of the past several years—and each year she has failed to reach her goal. Every year she hits the ground running and by midyear is on-track to hitting her goal. And then she hits the proverbial wall. She will tell you that it is because business always slows down in the summer for her. But I will tell you that it is more likely her "fear of success" that is slamming her into that wall. You can hear it in her voice. I can only imagine what is running through her head (I do not work with her directly, so I don't get to pry as much as I would like to!).

My thoughts are that she is thinking something like this: "What if I do make my goal? What will everyone think of me then? Will I still get to live in this comfortable level of production I have created for myself or will they expect me to do more? What if I can't do more? What if people expect me to do this *every* year? How will I ever do that? What if they expect me to *grow* my level of production year after year? I can't keep that up! It's too hard! Maybe I should just fall a little short of hitting my goal this year. That should take some of the pressure off. Then people won't expect so much from me. Yeah, that's what I'll do. I'll let my foot off the gas just a little bit. Not too much, but enough to keep people from pushing me so hard. That's it, it's perfect. I'll just keep doing what I've always done … I'm a decent producer … and what's more, I am *comfortable* right where I am!"

Can you see how this negative self-talk is keeping her from growing? How her fear of success is causing her to stay in the exact place she has been for years? Here is the real question: Do you find yourself having conversations like this in your own head? If the thought of accomplishing something makes you fearful of the "what then," I encourage you to take a closer look at what exactly you are afraid of.

Success can be scary. For many people, there is a certain degree of uncertainty in our accomplishments—wondering what will come next; wondering if we will be able to handle all the things that come along with having accomplished our feat; even wondering what our family, friends, and associates may think. These are all reasonable things to think about—but it is NOT reasonable to let them hold you back. If you are one of the people who find a fear of success is keeping you from moving forward, I want you to do the following:

....

- Write your goal in your journal.
- Beside that goal, write out the "self-talk" conversation you are having inside your own head. Be thorough—write down every thought or question you are having.
- Then take these thoughts/questions one by one and rationally think them through. If they involve another person, talk to that person. Share your concerns with that person. If you fear that accomplishing something at work will cause your boss to pile too much work on you, talk to your boss about the projects *you* would like to take on once you hit your goal. If you are afraid of how your friends and family will react to your taking that huge promotion (and its associated pay bump), talk to them about it. More often than not, you will find that with open and clear communication, people are more on your side than you thought—they may just have some fears of their own (such as that you no longer have time for them!). We spent Chapter 6 talking about surrounding yourself with the right people. When you do, you will find that you should *never* fear success—because the *right* people will always be there to support you!

....

Girls … victories are hard enough to come by. Claim your accomplishment. You've earned it! Furthermore, success breeds success. The more you accomplish in your life, the more you can look forward to accomplishing. Have you ever looked at someone and thought that "she *always* does great things" or "she *always* hits her goals"? Of course she always hits her goals. She has made a pattern of success, a "habit," if you will, of success. One of my best girlfriends is like this. She hits every goal she puts her mind to accomplishing. She is one of those people who set a goal and just go after it. No fear of failure (or at least not one that is evident to the rest of us) and absolutely no concern with the levels of success that will surely come to pass in her life. She just creates good habits and (to quote the country boys down South) "gets 'er done!" You go, girl – I can't wait to see the great things that lie in store for your future!

Each of you can do the very same thing. There are so many people in the world without your talent or your opportunities … don't waste your gifts on a life where you are scared to be the success that I (and you) know you can be!

Fear of taking risks

Yet another area where we see fear creeping in is in the area of taking risks. How many of you would consider yourself a risk taker? Someone who just goes after it … ready and willing to try anything that comes her way? NOT ME! I would say I am probably one of the biggest chickens on the planet … or at least I thought!

I was asked in a job interview once if I considered myself to be a big risk taker, to which I immediately replied "No." I went on to explain that I took calculated risks but that I typically did not do anything too risky (not sure if it was the answer he was looking for, but it did start a great conversation). During our conversation, the interviewer (who later became my managing partner … hey, I guess I answered the question OK after all!) completely reframed the way I look at taking risks. I had always thought of risk taking as doing those crazy, off-the-wall things that can get you killed … sky diving, bungee jumping, swimming with sharks. But what he did in this conversation forever changed the way I look at risk. He explained that taking risks did not always have to include dangerous things. That more frequently, it was simply addressing the unfamiliar— doing things that are out of your comfort zone. Things you had not, up until that point, attempted. He told me that my looking at making a career change was a risk and that having moved to a new city was an even bigger risk. (Hey, looks like I'm a risk taker after all ... although you'll find me *nowhere* near the open door of a prop plane ... I much prefer my flights with a Diet Coke and a bag of trail mix, thank you very much!).

How much a risk taker are you? Which of the following have you done? Whether it turned out to be a success or a failure is irrelevant. Remember that the key here is that we are working to overcome our fear of taking risks:

○ Moved to a new city (especially one devoid of family and friends)
○ Made a career change (either inside or outside your industry)
○ Started a business (This one's a risk, no matter which way you slice it!)
○ Gotten married (I mean, tying yourself to one person for the rest of your life ... what could be more risky?)
○ Let your mother (or your mother-in-law) have input into planning your wedding!
○ Had children (OK, maybe this one's more risky than marriage ... we've all been through the "joys" of childbirth ... big head ... little birth canal ... need I say more? And without knowing exactly what we were going to get! I've seen some awful children out there ... not yours, of course ... yours are all well-mannered, gifted angels ... I meant those *other* kids!)
○ Wore a bikini on vacation after having the kids mentioned above (I live near a beach ... this is a HUGE risk some people are bravely tackling ... whether they are succeeding is a *much* different story!).

You see, we are all risk takers to some degree. The challenge is to take each new opportunity as it comes and not let the fear of taking a risk keep us from doing something that could have a profound impact on our lives. There is a degree of risk in most things that are worthwhile—if not, everyone would be doing them. The people who reach great levels of success in this world are the people who are willing to try new things.

They are the people who continually step outside their comfort zone and try things others are unwilling to attempt.

When was the last time you took a big risk, one where you succeeded and it had a profound impact on your life?

_____

_____

_____

_____

Imagine what your life would be like had you not taken that risk. Now imagine a life where you readily take risks—not uncalculated risks, not ones where you jump in without even thinking, but risks where you are making a choice to move forward. Just think of all you could accomplish!

I don't want you girls running out trying every risky behavior out there. My challenge to each of you is that you work to remove "fear" when it comes to taking risks. Do your homework and research what's at stake. Look at all possible outcomes (this is where a good ol' "pros and cons" T-chart can come in handy!). Don't fall victim to "analysis paralysis," whereby you spend so much time thinking about and analyzing what's involved that it actually keeps you from moving ahead with anything. Weigh your options and then move forward with the confidence that, whatever happens, you went after what you wanted and what you believed in.

There is one additional tool that will be a huge help to us women in the area of risk taking. One with which the men in our lives are not as well-equipped … our "intuition" (you thought I was going to say "brains," didn't you?). As women, we have the gift of having a keen intuition … a gut feeling that rivals no other! Each of us has heard the countless stories about the woman who sensed that she was being followed and therefore walked right back into the store she had just exited or the woman who sensed that someone was in her apartment, so she immediately left and went to a neighbor's house to call the police (we get these types of stories e-mailed to us all the time by friends warning us to trust our instincts). Trust your gut. Do your research so you aren't going into things blindly, but trust your gut along the way. If you have a bad feeling about the person you are about to go into business with, think twice before you make a move … trust your gut!

When it comes to taking risks, don't be afraid. Trust that your analysis of the risk at hand combined with your keen intuition will lead you in the right direction. And if it doesn't, you'll live to fight another day!

Procrastination

So, on we move to yet another thing that tends to hold a lot of us back … procrastination (do you like how I saved this one till the end of the chapter!). This is one of the most common mistakes women make in their lives. Putting off doing things that need to be done until the very last minute: starting that huge project at work just days before the deadline, buying Junior's Halloween costume two days before Halloween (when you know that all of the good costumes are already gone!), waiting to clean the house until an hour before your in-laws arrive for a visit. Anything ringing a bell? Successful people act … they don't wait for things to happen. Your project will not miraculously complete itself, just as Junior's costume will not deliver itself to your doorstep and the mess in your house will not magically disappear into the floor! You have to go out and make these things happen.

I have no doubt that as working moms, who are proficient at multi-tasking, you have learned to excel at completing things at the last minute. My question is this: Why would you want to? Why would you want to give yourself the added stress of cutting things too close? The answer is simple: either you are putting off things because you don't want to do them or you are so scared of them that you are hoping they will just go away. Perhaps you are disorganized and have not created a system that will allow you to get everything done, well in advance of their deadlines.

Let's start with the first one—that you just don't want to do it! Frequently this form of procrastination shows up with things such as cleaning the house and packing for a trip. Or at work it comes with completing reports or making some dreaded phone calls. Whatever the item is, you put it off because you just don't want to do it in the first place. Come on! Have any of these things miraculously dropped off your to-do list just because your didn't want to do them? Of course not! Why then do we put off doing these items in hopes of them vanishing? Quite frankly, because we're acting like idiots! We are acting as though by sweeping the problem under the rug, it will go away! But it won't.

The minute you realize that these things will still be there and that you are creating more stress for yourself by putting them off is the minute you will release yourself from A LOT of undue stress. It's like ripping off a Band-Aid. The more you agonize over it and the more time you take to rip the sucker off, the worse it is. All moms know that when it comes to Band-Aids (and to all those unwanted to-do items), it's 1- 2- 3- Go!

Let's take a look at the things you have a tendency to put off. Make a list of the things you typically find yourself doing at the last minute, in either your personal or professional life.

* _____

* _____

* _____

* _____

* _____

Look back over this list. How many of these are things that are either mundane or boring or are things that scare you? Chances are … all of them. Conversely, how many of them are things you absolutely love to do? The answer is … NONE OF THEM! Because, if they were, they would be the things you did first! We can't love everything we have to do every minute of every day. There are going to be some tasks that are the "necessary evils" of our job and our life. These things still have to get done. So quit stressing yourself even more by putting them off, and either hire someone to do them for you … or get off your lazy booty and do them yourself … sometime before the eleventh hour!

I know I sound harsh, but ladies … this is an easy one. Once you tackle the things you have been putting off, you will not only free your calendar to do the more important and more fulfilling things, but you will also free your mind of the stress created by that nagging task lingering at the back of your mind. Take the items you listed above as items you *consistently* put off and write them down in your journal. Flag the page so that you can refer to it often. Continually look at that list, each and every day, to make sure you aren't actively putting off any of those items. If one of them is on your to-do list, rip off that Band-Aid and knock it out first thing so that you can get to the good stuff. Get in the habit of doing the things you don't like to do first. Or doing the necessary but hard (or scary) things first. You will have such a desire to get to the items you are passionate about that you will work extra-hard and will end up crossing that nagging item off in no time flat. Keep your list handy until you have built the "habit" of ripping off that Band-Aid.

But what if that's not the reason for your procrastination? What if you have no problem ripping off the proverbial Band-Aid but are simply disorganized and haven't developed a system for getting things done? That, my friends, we can fix. Just as we charted our course and developed a system for fitting everything in as it relates to the seven major areas of our lives, we will do the same here.

Look back at the items you listed above as items you have a tendency to put off. First things first: look to determine if there is anyone these items can be delegated to (whether they are personal or professional items). If you know you have a tendency toward putting these items off and that doing so creates more stress for you, why not offload them to someone else? This may work for a couple of the things on your list, but what about the others? How do we attack them and stop the pattern of procrastination?

Let's again start by keeping the list of these items in front of us. You've already written them in your journal. Now keep them in front of you at all times. Have your journal handy or, better yet, write out a list of your to-dos for the day or the week. Chances are you are probably doing this already. At the start of each day, decide which items you need to tackle first and do them … before moving on to anything else. Then cross them off your list (doesn't that feel good). Whether you keep your to-do list manually or on your PDA, refer to it often—prioritize the list—and don't deviate from it. Tackle each item as it comes and then move on to the next one. Just as above, this will help you more readily move on to other important and necessary items!

We have covered a TON in this chapter, and some (or all) of these issues will still creep up from time to time, but realize this: YOU have a CHOICE in letting these areas hold you back. YOU have a CHOICE in how you react when these situations creep into your life. You have *always* had the CHOICE … now, I am giving you the tools to help combat them. Don't waste this opportunity. Don't let yourself fall back into the "habit" of letting these areas rule your life. At the beginning of this journey, you made the decision to go after a more fulfilled and passionate life … one in which you are creating the life you desire … don't let off the gas now!

My challenge to each of you is to keep your journal handy. Write in it every time you see yourself falling victim to these roadblocks. Date you entries. Give full details. And consciously work to recognize these areas quickly and to remedy them even more quickly. Then watch as your entries get fewer and fewer … the dates for the entries further and further apart. Pretty soon, you will be asking yourself how you ever fell victim to these traps in the first place!

This chapter's checklist is pretty straightforward.

CHECKLIST

○ Buy yourself a journal (small enough to throw in your purse or your work bag ... yet sassy enough to look really cool when you're writing in it. After all, we have to look fabulous while we're empowering ourselves!)

○ Share your typical "problem areas" with your accountability partner (not your hips, thighs, and abs, but rather the problem areas outlined in this chapter ... we'll get to the thighs later!)

○ Be diligent about keeping your journal. Write down the times when you fall off the wagon, so that you can learn from them and not repeat the same mistakes ... that is until there is nothing to enter into it at all!

Chapter 9

LOOK AT THAT POWER

"Presence is more than just being there."

— MALCOLM FORBES

WE'VE HEARD IT ALL BEFORE ... "YOU NEVER GET A SECOND CHANCE TO MAKE A FIRST IMPRESSION." All our lives we've been told how important first impressions are. They shape what others think about us. They create an image in people's minds of who we are, how we might act, how smart we are. So why then does it seem like we are always trying to impress people ... like we have to continually live up to the "first impression" fame? The answer is simple ... because we do.

Regardless of what you may think, or what people may say, people's impressions of us DO matter, and how we look, dress, and groom ourselves are key factors in their forming these impressions. Don't get me wrong. I too subscribe to the "it's what's on the inside that matters most" mantra. However, and this is a big HOWEVER ... that does not give us license to roam around not caring how we look. Because (and I am sure I will be chastised for this one) ... looks DO matter. This doesn't mean we all need to look like Victoria's Secret models (not that I wouldn't trade my extra little bit of cushion for any one of their figures). What I am stating is that we need to look OUR best at all times. Put OUR best foot forward and always strive to create the best impression WE can. This will help create the powerful presence we need to be a success in the workplace and in life.

When you think about women who have powerful presences, who comes to mind? Perhaps Oprah Winfrey … Hillary Clinton … Barbara Walters … Angelina Jolie. These are all people who command attention when they enter a room. They are figures people look to for advice. You want to hear what they have to say. Now think of how each of these individuals puts *her* best foot forward. Have you ever seen them going into a meeting or making a TV appearance looking less than their best? Or entering a situation not caring what kind of impression they may make on those they come in contact with? The individuals listed above shape the lives of people they come in contact with every day. They have made it a part of themselves to put their best foot forward … to create a powerful presence that people naturally and genuinely want to emulate … and to do this every day!

I realize most of you may not have audiences as large as Oprah's or Barbara Walters' and may not be appearing before the U.S. Senate; however, each of you DOES have people you influence or are trying to influence. Perhaps it's the managers in the company you run, the employees you oversee, or your own family and friends. Each of us has groups of people we are attempting to influence—and the higher we climb up that corporate ladder, the larger the number of people we must influence and the more powerful presence we must possess.

How do we, as women, create that powerful presence without losing who we are? First, we must examine all the areas that make up our presence or our "image" and determine if they are working in our favor or if they are keeping us from projecting the image we desire. In this chapter, we are going to tackle some of my favorite topics as they relate to creating a powerful presence: crying, language (specifically the "naughty words"), attire, hair, and makeup. Now, before we dig in, I must say I am very excited about this chapter for a number of reasons. First, let it be said that throughout my career I have probably made ALL of the faux pas that I will cover in this section. Second, I (like many women I know) am always happy to take any opportunity to discuss hair, makeup, and fashion. And, since I do not possess the necessary talent to become the next Dolce &

Gabbana, I have to limit my fashion advice to how it might affect the working mom.

Let's tackle these issues one by one.

Big Girls Don't Cry ... (at least not at the office)

Let's start with the biggie: crying. I'd like you to take a minute and answer this simple question: *Have you ever shed a tear in the workplace?*

○ Yes   ○ No

Now, if we are all being honest, I would venture to guess that 98 percent of you answered "yes" to that question (and that an additional 1.95 percent of you are lying through your teeth!). Crying is a normal response to an emotional event. It's a reflection of the caring, compassionate beings we are. However, when it's done in the workplace, it can have an effect on the image we are trying to project. I am in no way saying to suck it up when you get a phone call that a dear friend has passed away or if you have a seriously ill family member. I am referring to the times when our emotions get the best of us and we just "lose it." Admit it: throughout your career there has likely been a time when you just lost it. When you reached the absolute maximum capacity for what you could take, and it all came flowing out.

I want you to think back to a time when this happened to you (and if you cannot think of a time related to you, try to think of a time you saw an associate have a meltdown). Take a minute to write down what happened and how you (or your associate) felt.

Read back over what you wrote. These are very real feelings and feelings that have merit. In most cases, you had every right to feel the way you did and it's all right that you got emotional … especially about things you hold dear … things you are passionate about. What I want to stress here is NOT that these aren't real feelings and NOT that you shouldn't have these feelings. The point is that, like it or not, having these meltdowns in a professional setting *can*, and often *does*, have an effect on how others perceive us in the workplace. I do not think this is right. I feel there is a double standard when it comes to this, but the fact remains that we must be aware of and conscious of how we are perceived if we want to create the powerful presence we desire.

Let's look at a real-life example: my example. As I mentioned, for years I worked in an extremely male-dominated industry. In such an industry, the majority of management teams are male-dominated, with a few of us females sprinkled in for good measure. It was in a meeting with such a group that I began to notice the double standard as it relates to this whole crying thing. Like most leadership teams, we had very successful individuals in the group, ones who had benefited from a lot of growth both personally and professionally. Our group prided itself on being authentic in leadership and in our lives. We always encouraged one another to be open and honest in our meetings and applauded one another for expressing our feelings … BUT… there was definitely a double standard. I do not feel it was in any way intentional on the part of the men in the group; I simply feel it existed, likely without their knowledge (now there's a shocker—the men in our lives not noticing something that is happening right under their noses!).

The double standard is this: when the men in the group expressed themselves to the point of showing emotion and shedding a tear, they were applauded for being true to their feelings, for being authentic, and for opening up. When I, as a female member of the group, did the same, the men didn't quite know how to react. It was almost as if they immediately felt that I'd been "broken" and that I needed them to "fix me." After all, that's what guys do, right? … They fix things. It was hard for them to see me as simply being authentic, as they did with one another. They saw instead this woman who had been reduced to tears. It was then that part two of the double standard kicked in. The first part was that they tried to fix the situation; the second was that now, instead of seeing me as authentic, they viewed me as being a bit weaker. I want you to refer back to the example you cited above. How were you (or your associate) treated once you had the meltdown? Do you think it helped or hurt your image in the eyes of those around you?

Another example of this played out in the political arena during the 2008 Democratic primary campaign. Hillary Clinton, during one of her campaign speeches, got a tad emotional. No serious weeping—she just got a little misty-eyed. When the TV political correspondents discussed it, there were several takes on the "emotion" she displayed. The majority of individuals polled felt it made her appear more human and in touch with everyday people. Which is exactly what we would expect from them. Everyday people cry. Everyday people express emotion. However, that wasn't the opinion expressed by the government leaders and people of power who were interviewed. They made it sound like she had had a moment of weakness—like she, as a leader, should not have shown herself to be vulnerable.

Personally, I think that is pathetic. I feel we should all be able to express whatever emotion comes our way, be we male or female. Why then am I ranting about this double standard? Simply to say we all need to know it exists. Right or wrong, each of us must be aware of this so that we can make a conscious decision about how to react when situations like this arise in a professional setting. I am not advocating that we turn off our emotions at the office or that we hide our true feelings. I just want us, as powerful women, to think things through.

There are several steps we can take to avoid having these meltdowns—or as I like to refer to them, "come aparts"—in plain view of everyone. And, by doing so, we can minimize the effect these could have on creating that powerful image we desire.

First, close by in every office is the ever-so-handy bathroom … a girl's best friend in times such as these. The bathroom can provide everything we need to shed a tear or two. There's privacy, and in most cases there are no men in there (those of you with the new-age unisex bathrooms may have to find a secret one on another floor). And, most importantly, there are tissues and a handy-dandy mirror to check your eyes for puffiness and running mascara after the episode has passed. Admit it, ladies: Which of us working moms hasn't shed a tear somewhere along our trip up the ladder? If there is no privacy to be found in the local bathroom, simply slip out for a bit to "run an errand." Time away from the situation to think and clear your head will do wonders for you.

Lastly, it is imperative that you have a confidant, someone close to you to share your feelings and emotions with. This could be your spouse or a close business associate (although I would strongly advise against its being someone who reports to you or someone up the chain from you). Look for someone who won't judge or try to fix things, but rather someone who will simply listen.

Remember: it is perfectly all right to have these moments and to show emotion—just be aware of the image it may be creating for you.

So, let's translate this into action. What is your plan for the next time you feel a meltdown coming on?

_____

_____

_____

_____

_____

And, most importantly, my confidant is: _____

"Mommy ... Suzy said a bad word!"

Once again we're on a topic that I am sure will evoke some emotion and some controversy. That is, the use of profanity in the workplace. Before we dive on in, I think it's only fair that I remind you that I was raised in the South—and there are just some words that we young ladies do not use, especially in a professional setting! As you have seen throughout this book, I have no problem throwing in a choice word here or there for emphasis, but I try to do it sparingly ... when a point really needs to be driven home. So that the focus is not the language, but rather the point I am trying to emphasize. I would never use those choice words in written word within a professional setting and would certainly strive to not use them out of anger. That is where people get in trouble.

Also, I very, very, very rarely use profanity in my speech in a professional setting. (In my personal life, I try to limit it too; but, as my husband will attest, if I stub my toe or fall down—as I am prone to do—then "S.O.B" can frequently be heard amid my cries!)

Truthfully, I never realized that profanity was much of an issue in professional settings until I moved to the East Coast. Perhaps it was my naiveté, perhaps I was just working with a strait-laced group prior to my move to the East Coast (although with some of the characters I worked with in St. Louis, I seriously doubt that), but I was in for a *huge* adjustment when I made the trek east. In fairness, I must say I absolutely love the East Coast and the people living there. However ... I was *shocked* to see how freely profanity poured from people's mouths. Be it during meetings or even from the mouths of speakers as they gave presentations at events and conferences I attended. It was shocking. Even more shocking to me was the fact that many of these outbursts came from professional *women*. I am not saying it's all right for one gender to use profanity and not the other. I am, however, advocating that we should all carefully choose the words we want to use. And, above all, know our audience. It is critical that we are aware of the message we are sending with our choice of language.

I once attended an event where one of the speakers, a very well-dressed, articulate professional, delivered some very important information on the topic of financial security. Her content was excellent, she was obviously very well versed and educated on her topic, and yet she did not connect with the majority of the audience. What's worse, she received terrible feedback on her presentation from the attendees, as well as from members of the board of the organization hosting the event. Why? It was simply due to the fact that her presentation was laced with profanity. Not every other word, but a good twenty to thirty choice words sprinkled throughout her forty-five-minute presentation. That was all it took. What could have led to her making a great impression on a large group of attendees and generating excellent leads for her own business ended with her never being asked to speak to that group again.

What opportunities are you missing because you have inadvertently created the image of a "potty mouth" (as our kids like to call it) for yourself?

Don't get me wrong. Most everyone slips up every so often. We're adults. It's only natural. Sometimes we throw in a saucy word here or there for emphasis. That is OK. People curse (or, as we say in the South, people "cuss"). But this should not give us license to do it frequently. Just as there is a double standard when it comes to shedding a tear, there is most certainly a double standard when it comes to the use of profanity by women in the workplace. As women, we have to realize that we are NOT one of the guys and we should NOT talk like them to try to fit in. We are our own selves, we are professionals, and, partially by our choice of words, we are continually creating our image. Further, you never know who may be nearby and who may be offended by your choice words.

Let me ask you: Are your words creating the image you want? What are some of the things you may need to change related to your word choices?

_____

_____

_____

Now that we've talked a bit about the words you are using, let's spend a moment on the words used by others. This could apply to virtually any industry or company but is likely more prevalent in male-dominated industries. I have, on numerous occasions, been the only female or one of a very few females in meetings or career-related gatherings. In some of these groups, it was as if the men didn't even know how to act with a female in the room. It was like I had been transported and now sat right in the middle of a high school boys' locker room! Not only have I witnessed my fair share of profanity throughout my professional life, but there have also been some choice words I wouldn't even care to spell. Call me a prude if you like, but I do not care for situations like that at all. Mind you, I've heard these words all before (for goodness sake, I am married to a musician and frequently joined him while he was on tour, so there is nothing I haven't heard or seen before). The difference is that this was occurring in the course of my business life … in a "supposed" professional setting. I chose to be around my husband's friends (and believe me, I always worked to make them behave too!), but I did not choose to have my professional atmosphere resemble a meeting of frat boys!

So, I had a choice to make: I could either sit there and by my silence approve of what was being said and how the good ol' boys were carrying on, or I could speak up. I chose the latter. At one such meeting (I'll keep the organization and the individuals involved anonymous … no need to throw anyone under the bus), I asked the group for a moment to share what I was experiencing. I told the men that while I could certainly tolerate the occasional choice word for emphasis, their having taken it to extremes on many occasions not only was offensive to me, but, more importantly, detracted from the message they were trying to convey. I let them know that I felt they were intelligent individuals, with a lot to offer the group, and that they didn't need the extra offensive "oomph" to get their message across.

To my pleasure, they did admit that that particular type of behavior was simply how they had talked in professional settings for years, but that they *did* see the need to clean it up a bit. More importantly, I was now viewed as someone who spoke what I believed and stood up for what I felt to be the right thing (that's a great way to add to the powerful image you are trying to create). Did I have fears that I would be viewed as prudish or that they would feel I wasn't tough enough to "hang with the boys"? Sure. But think back to the values exercise we did at the start of the book. Integrity is one of my core values. I couldn't sit through something that I personally found to be offensive and still claim to hold integrity as a value. It wouldn't have been true to who I am as a person. Sure, they sometimes teased me about being a prude and jokingly used substitute words in place of their previous choice phrases, but I could care less. Hearing a few jokes about my non-tolerant nature was far better than listening to them carry on like imbeciles!

I urge you to stay true to who you are with this one. You don't have to agree with me … you may be someone who likes to drop the "p-word" from time to time (although … seriously, girls … manners!). Whatever your stance, I want you to recognize that people react differently. And people form opinions of others for different reasons. You are intelligent women who are succeeding in your careers. You don't need to use profanity or act like "one of the boys" to blend in. In fact, you don't want to blend in at all. Now is the time to take it to the next level. Set yourself apart. Highlight all that's exceptional about you. Show 'em why you've made it this far and why you'll likely leave them all in the dust on your way up (plus, you don't see too many Fortune 500 CEOs cussin' from the podium, now do you?).

WHAT is she wearing?

Let me say it again … looks aren't everything. But, like it or not, in the corporate environment (and in life in general), they do play a very active role. It would be nice if it wasn't necessary to comment on appearance in a book like this, but, unfortunately, it is (plus, selfishly, it gives me a chance to dole out some fashion advice … it's like my own little moment in the fashion industry). Some of us (and I won't mention any names here) need this section. I have seen far too many women walking out the door looking like there is no mirror in their entire house. Ladies, ladies … how do you expect to create a powerful presence for yourselves—inside and out—when you can't even pull yourself together on the outside? The key is that you must first make an effort to look the part of a powerful person, both at home and at the office.

Let's start with dressing the part of a working mom. To a large part, I think the whole "casual Friday" theme has really thrown us all for a loop.

It has made it very difficult for us all. In my opinion, it is much harder for a female to dress casually and still look professional and command attention and respect.

I realize that many working moms work in casual environments. However, for the rest of us, my advice in the area of attire is rather straightforward—and likely something you've all heard before. Never let yourself be too casual in the corporate environment. Dress for the job you want. If you are climbing the corporate ladder, dress a couple of rungs up. If you're a high-level executive, dress as if you were a CEO. Don't go too short with the skirts or too low or sheer with the tops, and you should be fine. There is nothing more distracting than a too-short hemline. I mean really. I know you have seen these ladies out there. Standing up on the train so that everyone can see up their skirt! Walking around the office instilling fear in everyone that, at any given moment, you might actually see a butt cheek! These are adult women—do they not look in the mirror before leaving home? I am assuming (well, let me rephrase: I am PRAYING) that this does not apply to anyone reading this book, but if by chance it does (or if you know one of the culprits), let me simply say, "Come on, ladies. We are working moms … not hookers!"

I am not advocating that to be a high-level executive you need to be boring in the way you dress. Actually, I think quite the opposite. Too often, when I see pictures of high-powered female corporate executives, I feel like they have lost a bit of their femininity. It's like they have tried so hard to blend into the corporate male environment that they have lost any semblance of what sets them apart as women. Despite popular opinion, there are no rules that female executives need to subscribe to a boring wardrobe to get ahead. Why then do a lot of women do exactly that? Why are some female corporate execs deliberately trying to look less feminine and less attractive?

Are you one of those women? I want you to take a serious look at how you present yourself in the corporate environment. Does your corporate attire reflect who you are as a person? Or are you trying to fit into some type of preconceived mold? I am going to go out on a limb here. If you are one of the women pretending to be less than you are and deliberately trying to dress less feminine, no wonder you're reading this book and seeking how to create a better life. You're not living within who you are as a person. You're trying to create someone new, someone you *think* you should be. My advice is this … be who you are, and no one else. You got where you are because of you, so let that be what continues to propel you forward. Don't be afraid to take a little bit of a risk.

As I mentioned, I love the fashion industry and follow all the trends (I probably spend more money on fashion mags than I do on business journals). And despite the fact that I own at least five black suits, I do try to incorporate trends into my wardrobe. Trends show that you are current and that you are keeping up with the times. Now, if the parachute pants we all loved so much back in the '80s (I had a very cool purple pair!) happen to come back as the next hot trend, I wouldn't recommend going quite that far. You can, however, plug in all the latest colors and styles.

Create a signature style. Something that sets you apart. Something that is polished and professional yet symbolizes who you are as an individual. Have fun with accessories, follow trends ... be you! Just do it while always being conscious of creating and maintaining the image *you* want. The key is to feel good and confident in the clothes you are wearing. The clothes in your closet should enhance the great person you are, not detract from it. For those of you in the fashion and entertainment industries, God love you. You guys get to have all the fun. Go crazy, be funky and cool—you get to take more liberties than the rest of us corporate types. For the other 95 percent of us, just follow the simple rules: dress a touch above what is expected, don't show too much skin, follow the good trends and skip the bad ones, and, when in doubt, go black (there is nothing a good black suit and a little black dress can't cure!). Above all, have fun and be you (unless you're parading around as a scantily clad little mama … then perhaps you might want to go back and read this chapter again!).

Take a look in your mirror. Are there things you need to do in terms of your own wardrobe or appearance? If so, what?

Mary Kay Ash, the founder of the Mary Kay empire, summed it up best when she said, "While clothes may not make the woman, they certainly have a strong effect on her self-confidence—which, I believe, does make the woman." Strive to look polished and professional … not sexy!

Look at that hair! And that makeup … Oh My!

Now, on to hair and makeup. I can't leave the topic of appearance without touching on this subject. I am without question NOT an expert in the hair department. For most of my professional career, and much to the dismay of my mother, I have had long hair (I do realize that I am a grown woman with children of my own, but that fact does not seem to stop my mother from expressing her opinion about my choice of hairstyle!). Not only was my hair long, but it was long hair that I refused to pull back. Which is exactly what the infamous "they" say we should not do. They say that if we have long hair, we should pull it neatly back.

Personally, I feel there is a very logical explanation for the fact that there are a lot of professional women in their mid- to late thirties and early forties continuing to wear their hair long and refusing to cut it into a more professional style. The answer is simple: they all had mothers like mine! They had mothers who, in the 1970s or 1980s, decided to take the beautiful long hair their precious little ones had on their tiny heads and chop it off into a Dorothy Hamill hairstyle. Do you remember Dorothy Hamill? That cute, peppy ice skater with the *extremely short hair?* My mother did this to me not once but twice—once when I was five years old and again in the fifth grade. It's no wonder I hung onto my long hair a little too far past my prime. I didn't get another haircut (aside from a trim here and there) until after my freshman year in high school, and that too was a trauma. The "bob" hairstyle had just come into vogue, so I agreed to give it a try. Problem was, my "I know everything about the best haircut for you" mother thought my new bob would look even better with a perm! I looked like a poodle! It was kind of a Gilda Radner do but poofier! We even had to go back to the salon the next day to have layers cut into it to calm it down a bit. It was awful. My best friend laughed, as did my boyfriend. And what's worse, a few weeks later that awful do was immortalized in my high school yearbook pic! To this day, I panic a bit when I enter the salon. Thank goodness for my current stylist. She has managed, for the most part, to get me over my fear of scissors, and I now have what even my mother agrees is a "somewhat" professional style.

The moral is this: look professional, whatever your hairstyle. And always look neat, clean, and well-maintained. Nothing too earth-shattering, right?

As for the makeup, ladies, I will be brief. Don't overdo it! We are working moms, not ladies of the evening. I am fully in favor of makeup. It makes you look fresh and like you have taken time to pull yourself together and put your best foot—or, should I say, face—forward. As moms, makeup completes that polished look—just do it tastefully. If you think you have on too much makeup, you probably do! And if you don't wear any makeup at all, I would give it a go. I am sure that I am ticking off all the feminists out there who subscribe to the whole inner-beauty concept. I agree that what's most important is what is on the inside, but it sure doesn't hurt if the package it is wrapped in is all nice and neat too. It has to be said … people just look better with a touch of makeup and color. Nothing too drastic, just a little something to make you appear a bit more awake and fresh (which, after chasing the kiddos around, is something we all need!).

How about hair and makeup? Use the space below to jot down anything you need to do in this area:

Another Item on My To-Do List … A Hot Little Body

This is a tough section for me. And, I promise you this, I am NOT the person who should be doling out advice in the physical fitness category. But here we are, and it's my book, so I am gonna give it a whirl. To help you fully understand the difficulties I have in this category, let me give you a little background. Throughout high school and college, my weight fluctuated, mostly due to the amount of pizza and Cheetos I was managing to stuff into my face at the time, or to the obsessive diet I happened to put myself on. But toward the end of my college years, I found my stride. And I looked pretty darn good. I was fit, I was toned, and my boobs stood up proud, right where God had intended them to be! I could pull off all the latest styles, no matter how tight or how short (and believe me, when I went out on the town, I tested the limits). I did a bit of modeling (nothing too big but, still, local stuff that gave me some great running-around money), and when "they" told me that I needed to knock off a few pounds, all I had to do was skip a few meals and I was right back to 117 pounds. Does any of this sound familiar?

And then, somewhere between my twenties and my current age, someone played a very cruel joke. Those boobs managed to fall a few inches down my chest. There are wrinkles in areas that used to be taut, and these little "bubbles" are creeping up all over the place (I refuse to use the word "cellulite"). The trendy outfits I try on in the store are no longer tight by design; they are tight because I am trying to squeeze my fat butt into the size I "used to" wear! What's worse, I have discovered what "back fat" looks like. Knocking off a few pounds to ready myself for vacation no longer involves skipping a few meals. It involves a month at the gym and three meals a day eating absolute crap! What the heck happened? What was it I did that angered the gods so much? And what the heck do I have to do to make it up to them?

My rant is simply to point out that as we age, our bodies change. And while it seems like a cruel joke, there is really nothing we can do about the aging process (unless, of course, you are blessed with one of those genetically thin frames that allow you to eat whatever you want. And to those ladies, I say … *the rest of us all secretly hate you!*). As we get older, we have to put more effort into keeping ourselves in shape. Into being physically fit. And while I am one of those people who absolutely HATE to go to the gym, I DO realize the importance of staying in top shape—from both an appearance and a health standpoint. My husband, Shaun, has grasped this concept well. He gets up every day at 6 a.m. and either walks or goes to the gym … and even with him doing all that working out, I haven't lost a pound! I thought marriage was supposed to be a 50/50 kind of thing!

There are no shortcuts here (believe me, if there were, I would have found them by now). You simply must put in the sweat equity. If you hate to go to the gym, sign up for an exercise class with a friend, or go for a walk or a bike ride with the family. Do something. How you look (and, likewise, how you *feel* about how you look) is completely up to you. If you need to do something, do it. Quit making excuses.

Perhaps one of the best quotes I have ever heard in regard to people thinking they are fat came from Tony Robbins. He was speaking to an audience about the excuses people make for looking the way they do, and for not exercising or doing anything about it. Tony stated that frequently he heard people exclaim that they weren't fat; rather, they were "big-boned!" Tony eloquently explained that bones aren't skinny or fat … they're just bones. Think about it—have you ever seen a fat skeleton? Then he said to these people, "You're not big-boned … you're frickin' fat!" So, for all you "big-boned" ladies out there (myself included) … put down the potato chips, get off the couch, and get your butt in shape. If you're going to live the life you've imagined, you've got to look the part!

To wrap up this section, let's answer one simple question: *Am I satisfied with how I look and how I feel?*

○ Yes   ○ No

If your answer is "no," what is your plan to change your routine? (Check all that apply):

○ Join a gym (please note: the membership alone will not get you there ... you have to actually GO to the gym ... trust me on this one ... I've tried).

○ Sign up for an exercise class (you may want to recruit a buddy to make it more fun).

○ Meet with a nutritionist to develop an appropriate eating plan.

○ Actually stick to the diet you have been on for the last month.

○ Make an appointment for a checkup with your physician (just to make sure there are no medical reasons for why you aren't looking and feeling your best).

These are simply ideas to get you started. The key, as with everything else, is follow-through.

A Couple More Things ...

Set yourself apart — There is no better way to create a powerful presence than to be remembered for doing something special. Something that sets you apart from others. Your challenge is to find what this should be in your life. It needs to be something you do on a consistent basis, something that lifts others up and makes them feel good about having you in their life.

For me, I have chosen to send handwritten cards and notes on a regular basis. A marketing coach I hired some years ago had me do this as part of the marketing plan she helped me create. And I absolutely love doing it. It puts a smile on my face to write out the cards. And the response I get is overwhelming. I have people calling me and e-mailing me almost daily to thank me for thinking of them and for taking the time to write. In today's hurried world, people don't take time for things like this. I get at minimum 100 e-mails a day (a lot of them spam) and probably at least five pieces of junk mail. That's just shy of 750 pieces of *impersonal* "stuff" each and every week. And I probably get no more than one or two items each week where people have taken the time to write me a letter or sign a card with a brief little note. Think of how you can set yourself apart. I keep a stash of various cards (for all occasions) and a supply of blank notecards in my office at all times. I try to send a card or note whenever someone pops into my mind, or when I have read of a recent accomplishment or promotion. Additionally, I schedule time to write out birthday cards and other notes that may be timely.

A former business partner of mine does what he calls a "drive-by" in the office on certain mornings. When he gets into the office, he does a quick walk-through of the office, stopping to briefly say hello to the associates and staff members of the firm. He may have a brief conversation with some of them, but the key is that he is visible. He is engaged in the conversation and in getting to know the members of his team whom he may not interact with on a daily basis.

> What is a fun way you can set yourself apart ... while working to connect with others and create your own personal presence? Give it some thought and jot your ideas here:
>
> _____
>
> _____
>
> _____

Let me see that smile — This is an easy one. When I go through my day, I see far too many people walking around with a sourpuss face. I am asking that you NOT be one of those people. The great thing about a smile is that we have an unlimited amount of them. My charge to you is that you give away (at least) one smile a day ... to someone you don't know. Smile at the person next to you at a red light or at the elderly person you hold the door open for at lunch. Whoever it is and whatever the occasion, you will feel great spreading a bit of joy. It sounds simplistic, but it is a great way to spread a little cheer in our world.

Be able to stand on your own two feet — One of the most empowering things you can do as a woman is to know, with utmost certainty, that you are capable of standing on your own two feet, both emotionally and financially. While none of us expects the unforeseen to occur in our lives, it does. People get divorced; people pass away or become disabled unexpectedly. And at times like that, you don't want to have to be figuring out how you are going to get through it all. Knowing ahead of time that you can take care of yourself (and your family) will give you much more peace of mind should something occur, and it will give you much more power knowing that you are in control of your future, no matter what life may throw at you.

Although it's been a few years, this is what I used to help clients in my financial services practice with every day. You would be surprised how many successful executives don't have all their bases covered! I won't go into too much detail on this here (as it is beyond the scope of this book); but I would encourage you, if you haven't already, to meet with financial and legal professionals to address the following:

- What would happen in the event I or my spouse were to die prematurely? Or become disabled? Have we reviewed our current insurance coverage to ensure that it is adequate?
- Is our property and casualty coverage up-to-date? (car, homeowners, boat, etc.)
- Do we have an up-to-date will? Who are the guardians of our children? Are there trust provisions for the kids? When was the last time we reviewed our will?
- Do I know where to find information on all of our insurance and investment accounts? Does my spouse? (List this information and keep it in a safe place. And let the key people in your life know where to find it.)
- Have I taken a look at my retirement picture? At whether I will be able to fund my children's educations?

There are lots of other items you need to address … this list is just to start you thinking. The key is that the more in control you feel over your finances and over the "what ifs" you may encounter in life, the more powerful you will be.

Putting It All Together

To sum it all up, look polished and professional, set yourself apart, and take control over your life. Look like you have not only taken time on yourself but have taken time to become the most powerful self you can be. Be strong, and, as Lance Armstrong would say, "LiveStrong!"

Let's take a look back. What did we accomplish in this chapter? For this chapter's checklist, we are going to do an exercise I use often in working with individuals and teams to improve performance. I want you to look back over the various sections in this chapter and come up with a list of the things you need to "Start" doing (such as going to the gym), a list of the things you need to "Stop" doing (like trying to pull off wearing an ultra-mini at the ripe old age of forty-nine), and a list of the things you should "Continue" (as with the birthday cards you meticulously send out).

CHECKLIST

○ Complete the "Start—Stop—Continue" exercise

START:

STOP:

CONTINUE:

○ Commit to revisiting this exercise frequently to ensure
that you are continually building a powerful presence
for yourself.

Chapter 10

PUT THAT CAR IN DRIVE

"The power to define the situation is the ultimate power."
— JERRY RUBIN

NOW THAT WE HAVE WORKED HARD TO CREATE A POWERFUL PRESENCE, WHAT'S NEXT? How do we go out into that big world and claim what is rightfully ours? How do we grasp hold of the power we crave?

In exploring exactly how to accomplish this, we will take a deeper look into three topics in particular: 1.) the art of shameless self-promotion, 2.) staying away from self-deprecating behaviors, and 3.) being definitive in your speech.

The Art of Shameless Self-Promotion

Let's start with the tough one ... the one that is not a natural pattern of behavior for the majority of us lovely young chicas: the art of self-promotion. We have absolutely NO problem whatsoever telling anyone who will listen about the gifted skills of our three-year-old. Admit it: you must have made your little one write her name five times for whoever stopped by your office to say hello. After all, the ability to write your name without help at the tender age of three is quite an accomplishment ... why wouldn't we want to show it off? Well, the same goes for all of OUR accomplishments. Why aren't we just as eager to talk about them? One of the best measuring sticks for leading a fulfilled life is being thrilled with what you are doing professionally. To move forward as far as YOU would like to go. And one of the best ways to do that is to make sure those around you realize how awesome you are (without thinking that you are a total conceited beeotch!!!).

Let's figure out how to do just that. Start by picturing someone you know who is a master of promoting himself or herself. Not in a boastful way, but rather in a way that simply lets others know all of the cool accomplishments going on in that person's life. Are you picturing someone? Now let me ask another question: Are you picturing a male colleague? Chances are, that is probably exactly whom you pictured. But why? The truth is that men excel at the art of self-promotion. They have no reservations when it comes to letting others know all that they are working on, or have accomplished. They aren't shy about letting the world in on all the awesome things they have planned. Certainly, some have mastered this better than others (and others sound like they are just being cocky). Nonetheless, the men in our world are, as a whole, far better at this than women. My goal is to teach each of you to excel at this as well. In fact, I want you to be better at this than the men in your lives. We are all accomplishing great things and going great places ... why don't we let the rest of the world in on it?

How do we do this? To help you learn, I am going to tell you about my friend Joey. Joey (as you can probably tell by the name ... a male) is the master of the art of "shameless self-promotion." And he does it with such ease. He has certainly accomplished quite a lot in his career ... and what is even cooler is that pretty much anyone he knows (or comes in contact with) can tell you this. They all know the projects he has done, the results, and what he has in store for the future. Joey himself is the one who gives them all this message, but he does it with such ease and finesse that it never comes across as boastful. And, what's more, once people hear his message and the enthusiasm in his voice for all that he is doing, they become his cheerleaders, his advocates. Everyone wants Joey to win ... and everyone is attentive when he is sharing all the great things he has in store.

What does Joey do that is so different? Surprisingly, it is something any one of us can do ... and do with ease. As you did earlier in our journey together, Joey became very clear about his passions and his vision for the future. And with this type of clarity came a great degree of energy and enthusiasm about what he does. Each of you will see that as you begin spending more time working in your areas of strength and passion, it is very easy to get excited … and that excitement is contagious … very contagious! When you share your excitement with others, they naturally and genuinely become excited as well. They want to hear more about what it is that is making you so happy and excited. They begin to ask questions about what you have going on. Then you share your story. You let them know all that you have accomplished in that particular area and what you have in store. If you are genuinely excited about what you are doing (which you should be if you are working in an area of strength and passion), this will come across. And voila … you have just created some advocates. THAT is the art of shameless self-promotion … getting others to enthusiastically do the promoting for you!

As I said, I learned a lot from Joey on this topic. Not only did I learn how self-promotion should be done, but I also learned that I had been in a state of virtually "non-promotion." For some strange reason, like many females, I felt that sharing my accomplishments was nothing more than bragging and that it would make others resentful. What I found was *exactly* the opposite. When I did not "brag" on myself, my accomplishments often went unnoticed (primarily because there was one of the guys touting *his* own accomplishments). And if you were to ask who the standouts were among my peers, it seems that the names most often mentioned were those who tooted their own horns—despite the fact that they weren't accomplishing any more than the rest of us.

We got to talking about this fact in my study group (of which Joey is a member). A couple of us were lamenting about why certain people had been approached, we felt prematurely, to be a part of my former company's leadership development program, while other more qualified candidates (a number of whom happened to be females) had been overlooked. The natural inclination from the women in the group was to play the ol' gender card, but Joey had another idea. He suggested that part of the problem was that the women weren't as good as the guys in promoting themselves. He told us, quite simply, that we *all* needed to get better at promoting ourselves. To tell people what we wanted and why we were qualified for it … and not wait for them to see it for themselves. Sure, we have to have the performance and the credibility to back it up, but it doesn't hurt to be out there ahead of the crowd letting everyone know that we're on the way!

One of the first areas I put this into practice was public speaking. I am one of those strange individuals who actually *love* public speaking. Give me an audience and a topic, and I am in my element. (It's an odd one, I know, but it is truly one of my passions!) I had done a good bit of speaking by this time, but it was mostly talks and seminars that fell within the normal course of my job, and nothing I had sought out myself. I had always received excellent feedback on the talks I had given, and a lot of people were telling me that I was good at it and that they could tell that I really enjoyed it. The problem was that I, *myself*, had not been telling anyone that I loved it and was good at it.

After the "Joey talk" suggesting we get better at "shameless self-promotion," I decided to give it a try. I let everyone know what my goals regarding speaking were. I started talking to colleagues and friends in various organizations about how much I loved public speaking and how I was looking to increase this in my professional life. I stated simply that I had done a good bit of it and really wanted to do more. I said people had always said they could tell I loved speaking to groups and that I was pretty good at it, and I asked only that they let me know of any opportunities they heard of that might be a fit for me. The key was that my energy and passion really came through when I was talking to people about my goal. And, very shortly, I began to have people approach me with various speaking opportunities—chambers of commerce, women's organizations, and various clubs. It was like magic. And it was so easy it was unbelievable. I simply let my strengths and passions speak for themselves, and people caught the energy. They truly wanted to be a part of helping me live out my passions.

What is it that you need to promote about yourself? Think of something you have accomplished in your professional life recently. What should you be sharing with others?

_____

_____

_____

_____

Next, outline how you plan to share this, with energy and enthusiasm, so that others are made aware of your accomplishment and will want to advocate for you. What stories can you tell about yourself to illustrate your accomplishments?

_____

_____

_____

_____

Now, what passions have you uncovered that you want to share with others? What are your goals for executing on these passions? How can you share these goals so others may be able to assist you in making them a reality?

_____

_____

_____

_____

Now that you have learned the "art," you will need to stay focused on the "science" of self-promotion, and that is that it has to continually be a part of your professional (and personal) life. I am not advocating that you walk around all day every day letting others know "I did this ..." or "I'm going to do that ... ." That would be a little much to take! You do, however, need to make sure that the key players in your world are kept up to speed on what you've done and what you have in store. It will be a challenge, at times, to remember to self-promote. But it is always easier when you work within your passion. Just share your excitement for what you have done and what you plan to do with as many people as possible. Soon, you will have an arsenal of advocates promoting right along with you.

Staying Away from Self-Deprecating Behaviors

Now that we have all learned how to build ourselves up a bit in the eyes of others, let's spend some time on how to NOT immediately break down all that we have worked so hard to build up. I am talking about the self-deprecating behavior we see so often from women, not only in the professional world but also in their personal lives. As we begin our discussion on this topic, I ask you to answer one simple question: Have you ever found yourself saying something derogatory about yourself, your abilities, or your accomplishments (even if in jest)?

○ Yes   ○ No

If you answered "yes" to this question, you are among the gazillions of women in the world who find it easier (and less threatening) to beat everyone to the punch and throw a little jab aimed directly at yourself!

If you answered "no," please go back and reread the question ... because either you have read it incorrectly or you are not fessing up to the truth! We have ALL done this (and likely continue to do this). And we can't learn to correct it until we first admit we have a problem!

What is it you are really looking for when you do this? The answer is simple. You are looking for someone to tell you that you are wrong! If you say to one of your contemporaries, "I have to be the worst manager in the company ... everything I do seems to be wrong," what is it you are really hoping to get for an answer? Are you looking for him or her to say, "You're right! You should probably go ahead and resign before they fire your sorry ass!"? No ... you are looking for exactly the opposite. You want him or her to respond by saying how wonderful you are ... and showering you with accolades and examples of all the great accomplishments you have had. Am I right? Of course I am. But this is absolutely the WRONG thing to do in the professional environment ... especially as a woman! Let me tell you why. Because ANY man who has spent ANY quality time with a person of the female species can see right through you. And will view it as a desperate attempt for validation ... and that, ladies, makes us look weak!

Why do I say that our peers in the workplace will see right through it? Let me play out a scenario for you, and see if it sounds at all familiar. You are at home with your husband and are trying on the third of five little black dresses, trying to find the perfect outfit to wear out for date night (stop me if you've heard this before). Hubby is sitting in front of the TV, and you walk into the room and exclaim, "This dress makes me look fat, doesn't it?" (I told you that you'd heard this story before). Now let's think about it. Why do we ask that? Is it because we want the truth, or is it because we want to hear that we are, in fact, NOT fat (despite having given birth a month prior)? The obvious answer is the latter. If we wanted the truth, we would have asked our ten-year-old, not the man whose entire sex life is dependent on how he answers that loaded question.

If that one didn't ring a bell, let me try another one. You are looking through a magazine and come across a picture of one of those hot young celebrities. You know, the one who seems to have won the genetic lottery! So you show the pic to your significant other and ask, "Am I as pretty as Angelina Jolie?" What the heck are you asking that for? NO ... you are NOT as hot as Angelina! And if he tells you that you are ... he is lying (unless you are one of the *other* celebrity hotties out there). I know there are a ton of gorgeous women out there. Probably a lot of you reading this book. But come on. Ask yourself what you are trying to get out of this. Does it really matter if you are better-looking than Angelina Jolie? NO!

The only time this could EVER be a relevant question is if you were somehow competing with her for a role in a movie. I am assuming that is not the case for most of us, so the only reason you would ask that question is for validation. You need to know that you *are* pretty—you need to know that your spouse is going to *tell you* that you are pretty. Everyone needs to feel validation, but when you ask these types of questions over and over again, you start to expect the same answer. You expect to hear that you are pretty and that you are skinny. And that has a tendency to make us a bit complacent.

After nearly fifteen years of marriage, and years of working on our own personal growth, my husband no longer indulges me with the answers I used to crave. Sometimes he simply refuses to answer the question. Other times, he doesn't even look at me while he answers the question … he will simply reply, while still looking at the TV, "Nothing you wear could make you look fat." How sincere is that?!?!? My husband, in his wisdom (and in his attempt to help me realize *why* I kept asking such questions), helped me understand why I was reaching so hard. We discussed this at length. Shaun said that not only was I looking for some compliments and validation when asking the "fat" question, but I was also looking for an excuse … a way out of what I needed to do.

And that is exactly what *you* are doing when you ask these types of questions, at work or at home. If you think you're fat, what is it you need to do? You need to get your lazy butt off the couch and go to the gym. But when your hubby tells you that you aren't fat, what he has really done is given you permission to put off that trip to the gym. Likewise, when your co-worker showers you with all those compliments you practically begged for, you begin to think, "I'm pretty good, aren't I?" And perhaps you don't try quite as hard. If you continually point out all your flaws, it's because you realize that, in fact, they are flaws … you just want someone to tell you that they're not! Stop magnifying your flaws. If there is something wrong, do something about it! If there's not, quit trying to make it into an issue!

As women, many of us have gotten so used to putting ourselves down that we don't even know how to accept compliments anymore— be it about our appearance or our work. How many times has someone said to you, "That shirt is gorgeous" or "I love those jeans"? And how many times have you responded with a "What, this old thing?" or a "Are you kidding? They totally make my butt look huge!"? Or have a superior at the office compliment you on a job well-done. How often have you responded by giving ALL the credit away or by saying, "It was nothing"?

It WAS something, or else that person wouldn't be complimenting you on it! Do me a favor, ladies, and stop this! Learn to respond with a simple "Thank you!"

I was hugely guilty of this myself until one of my colleagues called me on it. He is a very good friend, so he knows how hard I work and how much I juggle. One day, he was *trying* to compliment me on a particular accomplishment my office had achieved, and I immediately responded with how it "really wasn't me … other people had done a lot of the work." But he knew that already and stopped me mid-sentence: "Kristin, stop … learn to take a compliment. All you have to say is 'Thank you!'" It was a tough habit for me to break (as I'm sure it will be for you), but you need to make the effort. Now, when I start to respond to one of his compliments, he just glances at me … at which point I stop what I am saying and simply say "Thank you!"

We all need to understand that these types of self-deprecating behaviors not only make us look weak and needy in the eyes of others, but also may make us strive a little less to be the best we can be, and cause us to feel content with where we are. I challenge you not to let this happen, and empower you to rid yourself of these self-deprecating behaviors. Let's start by identifying the areas in which you find yourself exhibiting such behavior. Take a couple of minutes to note some examples:

Personal:

_____

_____

_____

_____

Professional:

_____

_____

_____

_____

As with many vices in our lives, the first step is admitting that we have a problem. And now, you have done just that. The key is to continually be aware of these areas and stop yourself before you exhibit such self-deprecating behaviors. Once you begin to catch yourself and stop the behaviors, you will be well on your way to claiming your power.

Now that you're not going to be spending quite as much time putting yourself down, what should you say and what should you do during all the time we've freed up?

Being Definitive in Your Speech

Let's start by being the strongest person you can be in terms of your speech ... both at home and at the office. Too often I see otherwise-strong professional women committing a huge mistake in that they are way too wishy-washy in the way they speak. They say things like "I *think* it would be a good idea to …" or "*Maybe* we should ... ." What the heck is that all about? Come on, ladies. It's time to just say what you mean and ask for what you want. With all the multi-tasking we have going on in our lives, we could use the extra time we'll create by being more direct.

This has certainly been a challenge for me throughout my professional life (and, believe me, I don't have it anywhere near licked yet!). But what helped me the most was having a friend who spoke up and let me know what I was doing. I didn't even realize I was beating around the bush and not asking for what I wanted. One day, my good friend and colleague Mary said to me: "Kristin, the only time I get really mad at you is when you don't just come out and say what you are thinking." She went on to tell me that she felt I always had a great gut reaction but too frequently spent too much time trying to "say the right thing" instead of just spitting out what I meant.

If you are like me, a true "GRITS" (Girl Raised in the South), it is inbred in you to choose your words wisely—always careful not to offend anyone. Always thinking before you speak. Well, after several decades I have finally figured it out … that is a load of crap! We are strong, intelligent women, and it is time to step up and say what we mean, ask for exactly what we want, and not waste any more time putting ourselves down or beating around the bush!

I want to caution you, though, not to take this definitive speech to the extreme. Being definitive means asking for what you want and being clear and direct in your communication. It does NOT mean overreacting to a particular situation. This is particularly important in a professional environment. Rarely, if ever, do people losing their cool do any favors in "claiming their power." It can be likened to the toddler in the middle of the toy store throwing an absolute fit. As soon as she doesn't get her way, she immediately throws herself on the floor, yelling and screaming and ranting as to why things are "just not fair." Do parents suddenly give in and say, "OK, sweetie, you can have your little toy"? Not if they're good parents. Likewise in the professional setting, it doesn't do us any favors when we rant and rave and carry on like a child. We may get our way (especially if we're the boss), but we do far more damage to our image than can be imagined. People now view us as a person who is "not in control." And who wants those types of people running their company?

I want to empower you to keep your cool. To be the calm, cool, collected one who is getting it all done and not stressing over it one bit (at least not on the outside!). Remember this quote by Thomas Jefferson: "Nothing gives one person so much advantage over another as to remain always cool and unruffled under all circumstances."

Ask yourself: When do I need to be more definitive and ask for what I want—in a calm, cool manner?

Personal (getting help with chores, taking a mom's day off, always giving in when it comes to friends):

_____

_____

_____

Professional (asking for a raise, suggesting a new initiative at work):

_____

_____

_____

Excelling at claiming your power won't come overnight. Most of these things aren't second nature to us and will take conscious effort and practice. But I've got faith in you. And once you've got it mastered, there will be no stopping you. This is a great area for your accountability partner to help you. Share the things you learned in this chapter with them. And then give them permission to stop you when they see you going against the things you are supposed to be doing. Let me warn you: it will be tough the first time your husband tells you that your pants actually DO make you look fat. But I promise you this: it'll force you to do something about it! And, once you feel powerful, that newfound confidence (not cockiness) will take you further than you ever imagined.

This chapter's checklist is a short one:

CHECKLIST

○ Update your accountability partner on the things you learned in this chapter AND on the things you have identified as areas where you aren't "claiming your power."

○ For the next week (or until you begin to notice them and correct them yourself), keep a list of the areas discussed in this chapter—the ones where you aren't claiming your power. Be sure to cite specific examples. Review this list with your accountability partner to ensure that he or she can continually challenge you to squash these behaviors.

IF IT AIN'T BROKE, DON'T FIX IT

"Don't sweat the small stuff … and it's all small stuff."

— RICHARD CARLSON

WE'VE TACKLED SOME BIG TOPICS THUS FAR: IDENTI-FYING OUR STRENGTHS AND PASSIONS, OUTLINING OUR IDEAL SCHEDULE, AND TALKING ABOUT WORK, OUR SPOUSE, AND THOSE WE SURROUND OURSELVES WITH. Further, we learned how to get out of our own way and to not only create a powerful presence, but also claim that power. We've got lots to do … so let's spend some time making sure we're focusing our time and our energies where they should be.

To lead a fulfilled life, it is imperative that you understand that frequently it is not the grand gestures that keep us from having the life we desire, but rather the sum of the little choices we make *every* day. It is the *little* choices we make in terms of our thoughts and attitudes that keep us in a negative state of mind and prevent us from achieving the life we desire. I am sure you have heard the quote "Life is 10 percent what happens to us and 90 percent how we respond to it." This simple fact is imperative as you embark on the journey of being the most fabulous career mom of all.

As a proud multi-tasking super-mom, I find that my life is WAY too full to waste any time on worrying about trivial things. This is a lesson I learned at a young age—a lesson I have to keep *relearning*, every time something new is added to my plate (which occurs, I don't know, about fifty times a day!). Some moms I know stress over the wrinkle in their kid's shirt, or the spilled milk at breakfast. Others stress over every minute detail of a presentation they are giving at work, or spend hours crafting the perfect memo—which will probably take all of two minutes for the recipients to read.

When I went away to college, my father bought me the book *Don't Sweat the Small Stuff* by Richard Carlson as a reminder to pay attention to the important things in life and not to waste time on trivial things. It was a great book, and I read it often. Yet, as a busy college freshman, I still managed to stress over absolutely everything—what classes to take, what my major would be, which sorority to join (major things, I agree). I stressed over whom to invite to our sorority's crush party and what to wear to that party; I stressed over how to wear my hair on Friday night. (In the grand scheme of things, these were all rather trivial things. Although I will contend that big '80s hair WAS a major thing at the time.)

And, because my father, in his infinite wisdom, knew that I would likely forget the lessons of the book, he ended every letter he wrote me while I was in college with the following: "D.S.T.S.S.A.R.I.A.S.S.," which stood for "don't sweat the small stuff, and remember, it's all small stuff." That was all he needed to say. A gentle reminder to keep the focus where it should be.

This simple strategy can go a long way in your creating a more fulfilling life. Let's start by clearing your mind and getting all of the petty little things that consume a good chunk of your time completely out of our way. Honestly, I would venture to guess that a vast majority of females spend way too much time on trivial things. Further, a lot of the females I know have a tendency to overreact when it comes to these trivial things. And it is this tendency toward overreacting that wastes valuable energy and can keep us from moving forward. Before you can begin to have it all, you must quit wasting valuable time and energy on trivial crap that in the grand scheme of your life means absolutely nothing.

In my professional life, I have sat through countless meetings where we spend way too much time discussing things that simply aren't that important. And frequently my colleagues get into heated discussions and debates over things that don't hold any significance. Whether to lay off some of your employees IS significant and warrants the necessary attention and discussion. Arguing over which color napkins to use at your company awards dinner IS NOT significant.

The same type of wasted energy occurs at home. How many times have you argued over what's for dinner? Or what movie the kids can watch on TV? One of the areas that used to set me off was the way in which the kids (and I am including Shaun in this one) "cleaned" the house. It seems like I would have the place looking pretty darn good—neat and clean, all polished and free from dust—and then along came the "tornadoes" that reside in my home to wreck it all! Most of the time I would just lose it. I can't tell you how much energy I wasted blowing up at them. Sure, a clean house is important, and I still expect them to keep the house clean each day (although it remains a bit of a test for my "domestically challenged" brood). The difference now is in how I react to the situation.

I used to fly off the deep end, ranting and raving about how I was the only one who cleaned the house and was the only one who had respect enough for our things to pick up after myself. Now, I don't blow up anymore (well ... only occasionally, when I have had a *really* bad day at the office). I have, instead, made a CHOICE to react in a more productive way. And to not waste energy stressing over the "small stuff." With so much else going on in our lives and in the world around us, there's no time to waste on trivial things or to waste energy on things we likely cannot control.

Two of the things I view as absolute wastes of time and energy fall into the area of transportation. It astonishes me when I see drivers yelling at the traffic—as if that's going to miraculously make the traffic jam ahead of them disappear. Or when I see passengers fussing and moaning when their flight is delayed due to a mechanical problem or to the weather—like they really want to fly through a monsoon on a plane that has a bolt missing from its landing gear! It's as if they expect the ticketing agent to turn to them and say, "I'm sorry, sir. We didn't realize that you'd be inconvenienced; we'll go ahead and grab another plane out of our little storage unit to ensure you get to your destination right on time." Seriously, people! Ask yourself this question: Are you one of those people? I am not advocating that you sit by and let things happen around you. If you can take another route to avoid the traffic, do it. If airlines can reroute your travel, let 'em. Just don't waste precious time and energy complaining. If you want the situation to be different, then *do something about it*! Ask for what you want, in a direct and calm way. This will go a lot further toward getting your way and toward creating a happier you … plus, think of all the extra time you'll save by not sitting there complaining!

Think back over the last month and list three things you may have overreacted to. If you are having trouble coming up with any, ask your spouse (or someone else close to you)—I feel certain your partner will have NO problem listing a few. (We don't have all day here, so if your partner is anything like my husband, you will have to limit him or her to only *three* examples!)

> OK, I'll admit it; *maybe* I overreacted...
>
> * _____
>
> * _____
>
> * _____

Now, think about how much time you spent thinking about, steaming over, or complaining about the items you listed above. My guess is that it adds up to a pretty good chunk of time.

Next, I want you to *visualize* what you could have accomplished in the same amount of time. Could you have finished a project for work, made a phone call to catch up with an old friend, taken the kids for ice cream, or taken some alone time.

> What I would most like to do with my *extra* time is...
>
> • _____
>
> • _____
>
> • _____

A full and balanced life is about the sum of the *little* choices we make every day. In the above examples, you made a *conscious* choice to overreact and to waste that energy, and you and you alone are the one who had to pay the price ... after all, it is YOUR time that was used up! Now, I will certainly concur that your husband should have told you his parents were coming to visit ... prior to ten minutes before they arrived! But that is not the issue. The issue is that you are using up valuable time and energy on something that you likely cannot change. Sure, you can ensure that it doesn't happen again; but frankly, you could accomplish that with a thirty-second conversation, as opposed to a thirty-minute tirade. I have yet to find something whose outcome changed as a result of my overreacting. All I have found is regret for the time that has been wasted.

So how do we combat this? If you are anything like me, this could be a tough one. You see, I am genetically programmed to overreact. And any of you who have met my mother or my brother (bless their hearts) can attest to that fact! So, for me, it takes some work. I am going to share with you a trick I learned some years ago. I came across this idea in an old issue of Oprah's magazine (I love Oprah's magazine ... and live by some of the ideas from that thing!).

In the article, the author, Suzy Welch, gave a simple yet meaningful suggestion. She stated that when you are faced with a decision or faced with a situation to which you must react, consider this: What impact will my decision have in ten minutes, ten months, and ten years? In doing so, she suggests, the decision will become clear. If the decision will have little to no impact in ten years or even ten months, it is likely not something you need to spend a lot of time agonizing over (such as arguing with your husband over whether you needed another pair of shoes). Likewise, if the decision you are making or the point you are arguing will have a significant impact in ten years (such as how much money you should be socking away for college for each of your three children, or whether you should attend your daughter's dance recital vs. meeting with that big client), then it is worth investing some time and energy. Above all, decide how important the things you are spending time on actually are to you, and invest time and energy in them accordingly.

Let's refer back to one of the things you listed above as being something you may have overreacted to. Now apply the 10-10-10 rule to determine if you still feel this item is important "in the grand scheme of things."

Is it really that important?

○ Yes   ○ No

As working moms, we are all busy, driven people. We set goals, we go after what we want, and we push others around us to do the same. As we continue to climb that ladder of success, we often forget to stop and take in all that we have already accomplished. We just continue on as we always had … headstrong and going after what we want. But sometimes this charging ahead is simply that … just us charging ahead … with no real thought put into what we are doing or trying to accomplish. We are simply trying to forge ahead and win. This is where keeping things in perspective and determining where things fit into the grand scheme of things become critically important. We have to be aware of where we are headed, have a clear path to get there, and then continually be aware of where we are focusing our energies. AND, we need to stop and take a moment to be grateful for all that we *already* have in our lives!

You need only to look at those less fortunate than you to see what is really important to focus on in life. Nowhere does this play out better than in the world of reality television. Now, I am not a huge fan of reality shows, but I have seen a number of them, and a couple really drive this point home. Let's start with one that, I feel, focuses its priorities correctly. I am a big fan of ABC's *Extreme Makeover: Home Edition*, and every time I watch it, I cry like a baby. Not because of the desperate situation the featured family has found themselves in, but rather because of the selfless things many of them have done. I have seen families who, despite having very little themselves, have welcomed additional children into their home, often children with mental and physical disabilities. I have seen a single mother who worked multiple jobs while earning her degree, all to provide a better life for her children. These are people in unfortunate situations who, despite their circumstances, have made the CHOICE to devote their energy to making life better for someone else. Talk about having an impact in ten years!

Now, let's look at the other side of the coin. There is a show I have caught only a glimpse of, yet the message has stayed with me ... out of sheer amazement. This show follows parents and teens as they arrange "sweet 16"-type parties for their precious little teeny-boppers. These are not your average parties. These parents spend hundreds of thousands of dollars on a party ... for a teenager! And in addition are buying the teens hundred-thousand-dollar cars and jewelry fit for a princess. Are you kidding me? These teens and even some of the parents (mostly moms) are having absolute meltdowns working with the party planners to choose the perfect decorations to make the day a success. And the teens throw tantrums when their parents won't agree to buy them the top-of-the-line car at the local high-end dealership. Talk about wasting time and energy on things that pale in comparison to what is really important in life. Do these parents really think that choosing purple balloons vs. red ones will keep their little angels from getting into Harvard? And will placating their teens with an extravagant gift help them appreciate all they have ... or will it make them just a bit more entitled?

I currently live in Fairfield County, Connecticut, one of the pricier counties in the country—so I am sure I have just managed to tick off a number of my friends and neighbors. But seriously! Who are we kidding? If you can afford to throw this type of party for your teenager, while still saving appropriately and making charitable contributions, then more power to you. And if your teen manages to navigate adolescence and early adulthood with a sense of appreciation rather than an air of entitlement, then you've done a good job. But I urge you to think about the example you are setting for your children and, above all, to try not to waste time and energy on trivial things.

Think in terms of what is really important when you determine where to focus your energies. I am in no way suggesting that you ignore decisions that must be made. You are a leader, both at home and in your career. You have to make decisions. What you do NOT have to do is spend too much time and energy on the minor ones. Instead, focus your energy and passion on what's really important … taking it to the next level and creating the life you want for you and your family.

Just like my dad used to write at the bottom of the handwritten letters he sent me while I was away at college (long before e-mail!) …

D.S.T.S.S.A.R.I.A.S.S.

If you have trouble not sweating the small stuff, there is a wonderful series of books by Richard Carlson, often with his wife, Kristine, to help you through. These easy-to-read guides are full of suggestions you can implement in a number of areas of your life. They have truly helped me, and I hope they will do the same for you. Tragically, Mr. Carlson died of a pulmonary embolism during a flight from San Francisco to New York, in 2006, while he was on a promotion tour for one of his books. It is my hope that the principles he put forth will help you in your journey of creating the life you desire!

CHECKLIST

Here are a few to-dos to get you started on the right path:

○ Outline areas where you have a tendency to overreact.
○ Instruct your accountability partner to stop you when he or she sees you "sweating the small stuff."
○ Help others learn to not sweat the small stuff in their lives.

Above all ...

○ D.S.T.S.S.A.R.I.A.S.S.

Chapter 12

A JOURNEY FULL
OF LAUGHTER AND
CONNECTION

"Laughter is the closest distance between two people."

— VICTOR BORGE

I HAVE TO TELL YOU … I ABSOLUTELY LOVE TO LAUGH.
It is one of my favorite things to do. No matter how my day has been, a good hearty laugh can make it all better. But how many of you take time every day to laugh? I am not talking a simple little chuckle here. I mean a good ol' belly laugh. The kind your toddler is famous for. When my little Mia laughs, you can't help but laugh with her. She puts her whole face and body into it. Her eyes get HUGE, and she just cracks up! They say laughter adds years to your life … at this rate, Mia is going to live to be 210! But really, wouldn't it be great if we all laughed like that?

In today's fast-paced world, we take ourselves WAY too seriously! We spend so much time trying to be perfect that we have little time left to have some fun. To just relax and laugh a little. In my opinion, there is nothing that signifies all is good in your life in that particular moment more than just cracking up. One of the best qualities (aside from honesty) you can ask for in the people with whom you surround yourself is that they make you smile and laugh.

In my house, we all have things we do, on a consistent basis, that we know will always bring a smile to someone's face! Since early in our relationship, Shaun has gotten a kick out of my uncanny ability to incorporate "Shaunie" into the lyrics of almost any song. You see, I love singing along to the radio. I mean, really belting it out. The problem is that I am an absolutely AWFUL singer … can't carry a tune to save my life … but I know all the words, and I've got enthusiasm to rival no other! With a musician for a husband you have to make it exciting (mostly to avoid the critiques that would surely follow my treatment of a standby Bon Jovi classic). So, I find a way to weave his name into the middle of a song … and I do it with gusto! And it cracks him up, every time! Recently, I even started weaving Mia's name into the songs when she is in the car, and she loses it. Laughing like there's no tomorrow. The difference is that at 5½ she really thinks her name is in the song. She'll say to me, "They said Mia. I hope they say Bailey's name." And when the next verse offers up Bailey's name, she cracks up again. It sure makes car rides go by fast!

I am not naïve enough to think that we can laugh all the time. But I also know that each of us needs to laugh and that far too few of us actually do. When you were a child, life seemed full of things to find joy and laughter in: playing outside in the rain, jumping in mud puddles, tickle wars with your siblings, or even just making silly faces at each other. Think back to the things that made you laugh until your cheeks hurt or kept you playing outside until your parents yelled to you from the front porch to come home for supper.

In contrast, think back to the last time it rained—not a huge thunderstorm, but a light sprinkle. My guess is that not only did you NOT grab the kids and run outside to catch raindrops on your tongue, but you instead started crabbing about the very fact that it was raining at all! Further, I'll bet you fussed at your youngest for stepping right in the middle of that big puddle in the parking lot. What would it hurt to let kids play in the rain (they can take their shoes off before coming into the house)? And, contrary to what your mother told you, pneumonia is not caused by playing outside in the rain. When was the last time you told the kids to "stop it right now" when they were well in the middle of a full-blown tickle fest or told them that their faces would "stick like that" if they didn't stop it with the goofy faces.

What happened to us? I know … you were just about to say that "things are different now … we're grown-ups! We can't act like that anymore." And I am here to tell you that's a load of crap (note another use of one of the "naughty words" for emphasis here!). But really, it IS a bunch of crap! Somewhere along the line, someone told us that we were adults now … and they took away our "fun card." Why? I am not advocating that you ruin your Manolos and your good black suit with a midday splash in the local mud puddle. But I AM advocating that you add a little laughter and a little fun into your week—both scheduled and spontaneous. We have to be adults (for the most part) when we are running a company or making major decisions in our lives. But that doesn't mean our entire day should be devoid of fun.

There is a quote I absolutely love (and am sure you've heard before) that really drives this point home. It is by Father Alfred D. Souza and says:

DANCE as though no one is watching you,
LOVE as though you have never been hurt before,
SING as though no one can hear you,
LIVE as though heaven is on earth.

How awesome would it be if we ALL lived that every day? I put this quote to the test as often as I can (you've already heard about my singing, but you should see my signature dance moves!). How can YOU put this to practice in your life? Let's start with scheduling some fun! In Chapter 5 ("Thank God for the GPS"), we charted our course by scheduling time for a number of categories including self, spouse, and kids. These are prime opportunities for you to get in a little fun and laughter, as well as a chance to connect with the people most important in your life. Let's start by listing the things you *already* do (or plan to do) to bring a smile to that pretty little face of yours!

Here's what I do for fun and giggles (baking cookies for the PTA bake sale does not count!):
- _____
- _____
- _____

We are all busy, accomplished women, running households and companies … we deserve some time to just let it all hang out! Whether it is date night with the hubby or a girls' night out, we need our fun!

I must be honest. When I first developed my ideal schedule, I threw in all the obligatory things I thought sounded good being in there … date night with Shaun once or twice a month, one-on-one time with the kids. It was all in there. And I did those things, for a while. And then, they just sort of seemed mundane—like another thing I was trying to check off my list. That is NOT how your fun time should be! I had to make a drastic change to the things I was doing—it's not enough to just go through the motions … these things should be exciting!

Too many times, I see married couples out on what appears to be "date night." You're easy to spot—you are the ones looking tired and haggard. You are all dressed up in your slouchy clothes, as though you put no effort into it whatsoever. The young ones (the "pre-kid" couples) are dressed to the nines with fresh bright faces and big ol' smiles! Once at dinner, you sit across from each other, barely speaking two words (unless it is running through the list of all the children's to-dos for the week), then you catch a movie and it's home to pay the baby sitter the $75 you owe her for the mere pleasure of escaping the kids for a few hours! How close am I?

If this doesn't describe your date night, congratulations … you are in the minority who has actually figured out the meaning of spending time together … not merely coexisting in a restaurant and movie theater! But, if this does describe you, then listen up. You will never know joy, happiness, and laughter on these nights out unless you learn to have a little fun! Date night should be about truly being with your spouse and connecting. And it should, at times, involve bringing out the kid in you!

Look back at the calendar you created earlier in this book and identify when you slotted time for your spouse or significant other. Now, let's take it a step further and figure out what you are going to do to make these times more fun and meaningful. And yes, you ARE still allowed to see the occasional movie … just make sure it is because you want to see that movie and not just because there is nothing else to do.

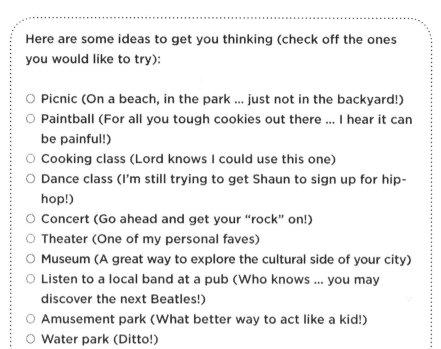

Here are some ideas to get you thinking (check off the ones you would like to try):

○ Picnic (On a beach, in the park ... just not in the backyard!)
○ Paintball (For all you tough cookies out there ... I hear it can be painful!)
○ Cooking class (Lord knows I could use this one)
○ Dance class (I'm still trying to get Shaun to sign up for hip-hop!)
○ Concert (Go ahead and get your "rock" on!)
○ Theater (One of my personal faves)
○ Museum (A great way to explore the cultural side of your city)
○ Listen to a local band at a pub (Who knows ... you may discover the next Beatles!)
○ Amusement park (What better way to act like a kid!)
○ Water park (Ditto!)
○ Wine-tasting class or winery tour (A great way to bond ... just don't get too tipsy!)

There are lots more ... just use your imagination a bit. The key is to mix it up a little. Don't let date night become boring ... make sure to include some spontaneity and allow plenty of time to smile and to laugh.

Now, on to time with the wee ones. Are you taking time to do anything special with them ... one-on-one? I had a colleague who has two sons, now both in their twenties. He told me that while they were growing up (once they were old enough to appreciate it), every Friday he would take one of them to breakfast before school (he'd take the other the next week, and so on). It grew to be quite the ritual for him and his sons. So much so that they still relish those father-son breakfasts whenever they can ... even though they are out of college! The key, he told me, was consistency. It was something they did every week. And his boys knew that they were the absolute most important thing to their father!

My colleague shared that some weeks they would pour out all their feelings and talk about what was going on in their lives. Other weeks (typically when someone had just gotten into trouble for one of the many teenage faux pas), there was little conversation—they just glared at each other across the table (they are males, of course; heaven forbid that they actually *talk* through their differences!). But they made time for each other … one-on-one. And they each knew, above everything else, the importance of those children in their father's life!

When I heard this, I immediately thought I HAD TO give it a go. School had just started up again, so Bailey and I had our first "Mommy-daughter" breakfast (although, when I called it a "Mommy-daughter" breakfast, I was immediately chastised by Bailey. Apparently, once children reach double digits, it is no longer appropriate to refer to yourself as "Mommy." That is WAY too embarrassing.)

What are YOU going to do to connect better with your kids? What kinds of things would be fun for you AND them? The key to creating a better life and truly feeling like you have it all is to be firing on all cylinders, to do everything in your power to make sure ALL areas of your life are nurtured (spouse, children, family, friends, career, community, and self). We want to leave no stone unturned.

So often we neglect building relationships with our children and spending time on things that are important to them. Too many moms have turned into nothing other than glorified taxi drivers and scheduling coordinators. Most kids today have very little free time in their schedules. They run from school to soccer practice to ballet and then grab a quick bite before hitting the books for a couple of hours. What happened to free time? What happened to just being a kid? Can you remember back to what it was like when you were young? Before the only exercise kids got was playing their Wii? Before cellphones and e-mail?

We lived simpler lives then, lives that let us actually enjoy being a kid rather than spending our childhood being shuffled from one lesson to the next. We played red rover, red light/green light, and king of the mountain. We stayed outside until the streetlights came on and Mom yelled at us to come home. We caught lightning bugs in a jar and caught snowflakes on our tongues. When did these times disappear?

Most children have not experienced simply "playing" like this. If they aren't caught up in the middle of their scheduled activities, they are on the computer or in front of the TV or they're playing video games. Let's claim some of this back for our children. Let's allow them to experience real play and creativity. Let's pull them away from the television for a while and let them breathe some fresh air. Let's stop short of scheduling every waking moment of their lives with a zillion and one lessons. Yes, I do realize that Junior has a much better chance of getting into Yale if he has mastered Latin (and Spanish and French) prior to the seventh grade. BUT Junior won't have any friends … or any hobbies! We need to work to make Junior a well-rounded person. One who not only is involved with lessons and activities that he loves and that will serve him well later in life, but also understands the importance of just being a kid!

Who among us wouldn't love to be a kid again, even if just for one day? To volunteer to help the teacher make copies (really, who didn't love the smell of the ditto machine?) or dust off the chalk erasers. Where we could just call a "do over" when we screwed up. Or to have the opportunity to do really fun things with our parents—like skating or playing in the park. Let me spell it out for you, girls … sitting on the couch watching television does NOT constitute quality time with the children … even if you do discuss who should have been kicked off *American Idol*.

My challenge for each of you is to find some way to connect with each of your children, in a way that is fun for them. In a way that lets them be a kid. Do a bit of fact-finding. Ask them what they like to do. Let them tell you how they'd like to spend their one-on-one time with you.

In my house, we have "palette night" on Fridays. We rent a movie, let the kids pick out a candy they like, and put comforters and pillows on the floor for a big slumber party (mind you, my kids are eleven and five … not so sure this would work with seventeen-year-olds). But the key is that the girls love it! They look forward to Fridays (and it becomes a great piece of leverage if they aren't behaving themselves). The girls and I also have great dance parties on some of the nights when Dad is traveling. We turn up the music … their music … as loud as we like and then dance all around the living room! They go crazy … and I get to count it as one of my workouts for the week! Now, c'mon, ladies … I know there are more of you out there who know every Miley Cyrus and Justin Bieber lyric … and would prefer some quality time with the kids to another trip to the gym!

You just have to be creative and make it fun. Get to know your kids. And at least once or twice a week, quit nagging them and just let loose. If you are thinking, "How in the world am I going to make time for this?",

I want to tell you one thing … you have to! And I don't want to hear any discussion on this. I know you're busy. I know you have a million things to do at home and at the office. But none of those million things is as important as your children—so make the time!

It's like another of my favorite quotes—this one from Forest Witcraft: "A hundred years from now it will not matter what my bank account was, the sort of house I lived in, or the kind of car I drove … but the world may be different because I was important in the life of a child."

Be important to YOUR children. Teach them well and be present for them. The people I come across who are leading lives full of joy and fulfillment take time for the special things in life: for family, for fun, and for laughter! So let's put the plan in motion. First, refer back to the weekly calendar you created. Look at the times you allotted for family/kid time. What are you going to do with that scheduled time?

Depending on the age of your children, here are a few suggestions (some may sound a bit familiar):

- Breakfast before school (Go to a local diner … breakfast at home doesn't count!)
- Picnic (Nothing beats PB&J on the beach)
- Theater (Gotta get a little culture in there … and the kids LOVE it)
- Museum (Same here)
- Amusement park (You'll have more of an excuse to cut loose with the kids along for the ride)
- Roller skating/ice skating (I still have my old skates in the garage somewhere!)
- Batting cages (This is actually quite a workout)
- Mini golf/Golf (I stink at mini golf, so the kids love beating me!)
- Swimming (Tough if you have an aversion to being seen in a bathing suit!)
- Manis and pedis (Tend to work a little better with daughters, but hey, who am I to judge?!?)
- Library/bookstore (Put that mind to work)

Aside from these structured events, I encourage each of you to focus on the spontaneous things you can do to have a little fun with your children (like the dance parties or tickle-fest moments). The less time you spend "sweating the small stuff," the more time you will have to actually *enjoy* your family!

There's one last person who simply MUST have some fun ... YOU! And this seems to be the one area we busy moms neglect. I spent so many years trying to make sure everyone else had some fun that I often forgot to have some fun myself. I think a lot of us make that mistake. We spend so much time putting others first that, except for the occasional night out with the girls, we take very little time to have fun! And I can't tell you how critically important that is.

When we first moved to Connecticut, we knew a grand total of three people in the entire state and I worked with all of them! I knew absolutely no one outside the office. One of the moms in my daughter's new school was nice enough to invite me to one of her Bunco groups so that I could meet some of the other moms in the school (I think she just felt bad that I had no friends!). Our group typically consists of sixteen or so moms, with kids of varying ages, looking for an excuse to get out of the house and have a few laughs.

If you aren't familiar with Bunco night, let me fill you in. It is the girls' equivalent of boys' poker night ... without any skills required! It involves dice, food, wine, and laughing until either your stomach hurts or you pee in your pants (both of which have happened at our Bunco nights ... I'll mention no names here, though!). I joined this group a few years ago and have since moved to a town about forty minutes away, but I continue to attend the monthly Bunco night whenever I am in town. And I wouldn't miss it for the world. Why? Because I have never laughed so hard in my life! For one night every month, we get together to compare notes, tell parenting stories, and just be ourselves.

Our group of "Bunco Babes," as we like to call ourselves, is the most diverse group of individuals you could imagine (we have stay-at-home moms, a nurse, a hairdresser, and even an alpaca breeder). But when we get together, our purpose is clear ... to act like a bunch of crazy women and to have a blast! One night a month, we don't sweat the small stuff. Heck, we don't even sweat the big stuff. We just enjoy being us!

My hope for each of you is that you find time to connect with the people most important in your life and that you take some time to laugh. Keep working at this until it becomes a habit. The joy you feel when you create those special moments for you and your family will be well worth the effort!

But all of this fun and laughter is likely to leave you a bit tired, so in the next chapter we are going to focus on taking time for yourself, just to recharge your batteries. We're going to ensure that you find your own "Bunco Babe" moment! In the meantime, remember: Life's too short not to make the adventure fun!

CHECKLIST

○ Outline your ideas for a fun date night- (your list MUST consist of more than simply "dinner and a movie")

○ Find out what your kids would like to do for their one-on-one time with you. Then schedule it into your routine.

····· *Chapter 13* ·····

MOM'S GOING FOR A DRIVE

"True happiness arises, in the first place, from the enjoyment of one's self, and in the next, from the friendship and conversation of a few select companions."

— JOSEPH ADDISON

THROUGHOUT THIS JOURNEY, WE HAVE WORKED REALLY HARD TO PUT THINGS IN PLACE AS WE WORK TOWARD CREATING A BETTER LIFE, A MORE FULFILLED LIFE FOR OURSELVES. Holy crap—we've done a lot of work! And when we've done a lot of work and need a break, ladies, what do we do? We take a little "me time!"

As the multi-tasking femmes fatales we are, we are always putting out a million fires, both around the office and at home. And all this taking care of others is really taking a toll on us (which is why some of us look like we're 50 at the ripe ol' age of 35!). We continually sacrifice for others and take absolutely no time for ourselves. And this has to change. NOW! I know countless women who actually feel guilty when they take time for themselves. As if every waking moment of their lives is supposed to be spent caring for others. If you are among this group of misguided ladies, I am here to tell you: your life is never going to be as fulfilled as you would like unless you first learn to take care of Y-O-U! This is a fact—and no one is exempt.

I know there are a number of you who have just read that and are saying to yourselves, "I put others first because I want to. My family and friends are the most important things in my life, and they come first." And you say this because this is the noble thing to say. Because for some reason you have decided that putting others first makes you a better person. And it does … but NOT at the expense of taking some time to just be … and to have fun … for no other reason than to make YOU happy!

The stronger you are as a person and the more relaxed and content you are with your own enjoyment of life, the stronger you will be for others. It allows you the freedom to be relaxed around others, to be present and engaged in your interactions with them. That type of interaction is what is noble … what makes you a better person. If you are wiped out from everything you are juggling between work and home and you have taken no time for yourself to recharge your batteries, you aren't worth squat to anyone else. What good does it do to spend your time taking care of others if you're a worn-out ol' mama when you're doing it? How strong it that? How fulfilled?

My challenge for each of you is to become that fabulous woman every other woman envies. The one who looks hot and full of spice when she's out on the town with her girlfriends for a fabulous girls' night out. The one who gives her absolute best at the office and the one who gives her absolute best to her family. And the only way to accomplish this is to actually stop and take some time for YOU.

Let's start with some self-evaluation. Two simple questions:

Are you taking enough time to just "be" and to be alone in your thoughts?

◯ Yes   ◯ No

Do you regularly have social time with a group of your comrades? (If the hubby and kids are along for the ride, it DOES NOT COUNT!)

◯ Yes   ◯ No

If you cannot answer an absolute "YES" to BOTH of these questions, I can assure you that you are not being the best you can be for others and you are absolutely NOT living as fulfilled a life as you can. How do you change that? Or how do you expand on that if you are one of the crafty ones who answered "yes"?

To develop a "me time" plan, let's start with the daily stuff. While the directive of taking some alone time each day may seem daunting, it really isn't. You don't have to sneak off every evening for a few hours to do something fun—it's not that at all. Taking some time for you each and every day is actually quite the opposite. It is not spending hours doing selfish things for you. It's not running to the nail salon or grabbing a bite to eat with a friend (we'll cover those later). I am referring to the time you take with the woman who should be your absolute best friend … your confidante … once again, I am referring to Y-O-U.

One of the common female mantras is that men simply "don't think." But I will tell you … neither do we! While we are great at thinking of the right answer to a problem, or the most efficient way to multi-task, we absolutely suck at thinking about what WE want out of our lives, or even out of our day. We take no time to just be alone in our thoughts—whether it is to reflect or to plan for the future. And solving this is really quite simple.

Most people have a bit of a commute to the office, or some amount of time they are alone in a car, train, or airplane as part of the normal workday commute (for my girlfriends in NYC, I know that cab ride is short and the subway allows no time to reflect—you may have to search a little harder for some alone time!). During this commute, I want you to do three simple things: 1.) Turn off the radio, 2.) Think of all the things you're grateful for in your life, and 3.) Dream of what you'll do next. Really take time to THINK … every day … about serious and meaningful things … about where your life is going … about where you dream it will go. Do NOT spend the time running through a mental checklist of today's to-do items or this evening's grocery list. That won't help you at all!

You don't have to do this every time you are in the car or every time you have time alone. But you should consciously make time *every day* to spend ten to twenty minutes alone in your thoughts. If the commute doesn't work for you, try something else. Be creative. On occasion, I take my "twenty minutes of Zen" at the tanning bed. Sometimes, it is the only twenty minutes of my day when the phone isn't ringing (or if it is, I can't hear it!) and no one is asking me a question! I know, I know … tanning beds are bad for your health … but so is vacationing in a tropical location with ghostly white skin (plus, everyone knows you look thinner with a tan!). The key is to make the alone time with your thoughts count. Most days, when I am alone in my car, I rarely turn on the radio anymore (unless I am psyching myself up for a big meeting with a client or on my way to a speaking engagement … then, there's nothing like a little Bon Jovi turned up real loud—with me belting out the lyrics—to get me pumped!). With the radio off, you are forced to be alone in your thoughts. And, once you train yourself to think of things other than your to-do list, you will be amazed where your thoughts will take you.

How will you make time for your twenty minutes of Zen? Where do you plan to find your "alone time"? Here are some thoughts (and feel free to add a few of you own). The key is to make it a seamless part of your everyday life.

....

- Early morning reflection or meditation
- Commute time
- Tanning bed moments
- Massage appointments (If you have managed to find time to get a daily massage, you must call me immediately and let me know your trick! Otherwise, this could work for a few days here and there.)
- Ten-minute power naps (the ones where you stop for a sec but aren't able to actually fall asleep)
- Bath time (nothing says relaxing and reflecting like a Jacuzzi tub full of bubbles!)
- After the kids and hubby are all "snug as a bug in a rug!"

....

Three quick follow-up questions:

Do you understand the importance of this in creating a truly
passionate and powerful life ... one in which you truly "have it all"?

○ Yes   ○ No

Do you feel you can make this commitment and fit this into
your everyday schedule?

○ Yes   ○ No

Will you COMMIT to making time every day for YOU, to just
"BE" and to reflect on and further envision the life you so
vividly imagine and desire?

○ Yes   ○ No

If you said NO to any of the above, quite frankly ... you've lost it!
Or you completely skipped the first part of the chapter where I went on a
mini-rant on why "me time" is so important. If that is you, please read no
further ... for you must go back a few pages and start the flippin' chapter
over again ... and try to pay attention this time!

For the rest of you, you're on your way ... and now comes the really
fun part ... the *mandatory* girls' night out. We are going to discuss the
importance of having some time out with the girls. This is the section
of the book that you will definitely want to flag for future reference. You
should highlight it and keep a bookmark or a little sticky note on this
page ... just in case your husband happens to pick up your book to see
what the heck you are reading. Then you will be forced to explain to your
mate that the talented and wise author, Kristin Andree, has told you that
to be the "it girl" who is at the top of her game, you simply MUST go out
with the girls on a regular basis! And, if he has any problem whatsoever

with that, just have him give my husband a call … I have him pretty well trained on this matter (and he will concede that it really does make for a more relaxed and more willing partner!).

I don't believe there is a certain frequency for which you must head out on the town (or head out *of* town). It will be different for each of you. You know best when you are feeling the need to "get away." The key is that you need to *listen* to those feelings. When you feel like you want to strangle your wee little ones, or when everything out of your spouse's mouth seems to grate on your last nerve, it's probably time for a breather. When work has you feeling like you're drowning and your employees have all seemingly turned into a bunch of idiots, you probably need to blow off a little steam. Sometimes you will want to go out with your husband; other times, with your family. But you need to make sure you have times without them as well, because, quite frankly, they may frequently be the source of your tiredness or frustration!

So, what's a tired, frustrated girl to do? First, you need to look at your circle: Do you have a group of girlfriends you go to when you want to have some fun? If so, count yourself among the lucky ones. So few of us today take time to really cultivate meaningful friendships with other women. After all, with working seventy hours a week and raising a family, who has the time? YOU DO! If we look at our lives, there is not one of us around who couldn't take time to build in a little "me time." You are a working mom, rising through the ranks of your company. You are in charge … for goodness' sake, claim your power and make the time!

So, who are your go-to gals? (list them here):

_____   _____

_____   _____

_____   _____

_____   _____

Once you have found your group of girls, plan some regular outings. (If you don't possess the social or organizational skills to do so, find the one in the group who does and simply say, "We should plan a girls' night." She'll be all over it.) Go to dinner, go to a play, go dancing. Or plan a weekend getaway, spa trip, or beach outing. The key is to enjoy one another's company. Inevitably during the course of an evening out, there will be some sharing of kid, work, and hubby stories, and you will learn that you are not the only one who feels like she is being pulled in a zillion directions. You are not the only one whose daughter insists she is "ruining my life." And you are, by no means, the only one whose husband requires more picking up after than their children. You can't get these types of reassurances from your co-workers or even your spouse. You have to hear it from those in the trenches with you ... the rest of the girls on *their* own girls' night out!

One more word of advice on your girls' time. Do it right ... and do it up. If you are tired of looking the part of the tattered working mom, walking around like a "shlumpadinka" (to quote Oprah), then don't go out of the house looking like one. Dress up, do your hair and makeup ... look fierce! Show some style ... add some flair ... make it worthy of a fun time with the girls. If there is nothing in your closet besides business suits and the jeans, sweats, and T's you wear on the weekends, it might be time to make a quick run to the mall. Build a stable of little black dresses—the fashionistas' answer to everything (and yes, it's OK to have more than one). Throw on some heels and fun jewelry. This is a time to recharge, and looking like a worn-out old hag won't recharge shit (note the use of a bit of profanity there ... a little bit of that "emphasis" I promised you ... just so you know I mean business here!). But really, how can you expect to have any fun or to blow off a little steam if you look like crud? If you haven't put any time into your girls' night, why should your girls' night put any time into you ... into giving you that much-needed boost of excitement and a little bit of relaxation?

By now you should know how attentive I am to follow-through. So, let's talk about it. How are you going to follow through on this? Before you move on to the next chapter, I want you to take the first step toward having some scheduled "me time." Look at the list of friends you outlined above and make some phone calls. Plan something. You can start small

… if you all have fun, it'll grow and expand from there. The key is to do something regularly.

Make your own set of invites. Here we go …

You're Invited:

What: Girls' Night Out

When: ASAP!!!

Where: Somewhere fun!!!

If you can't seem to get a group of your girlfriends together for some fun, look into other events you can do on a social basis. I assume a number of you executive types are involved in some sort of networking group or industry organization. Often these organizations have women's groups, and frequently those groups host purely social functions. This is an excellent way to get to know some other like-minded women. I have met some great women through these types of get-togethers. Now, I have also met some I wouldn't choose to go out on the town with. But the cool thing is that you get to pick whom you want to hang with. Seek out women with common interests, ones you enjoy being around. You can tell after talking with people for two minutes if you would want to spend any time with them socially. If you like them, let them know. Tell them you'd love to get together for lunch or coffee sometime. This could be the start of a great friendship.

You may have to do a little research if you aren't already familiar with organizations in your area you can involve yourself with. Ask around or do some Internet research to see what you can come up with. Once you've found something, fill it in here.

Here are some women's organizations whose events I should attend:

* _____
* _____
* _____
* _____
* _____

I hope this chapter has given you an opportunity to start thinking through some ways to add a bit more fun and more time for yourself into your already-jampacked routine. I promise you this: if you consistently take time for yourself and begin to cultivate things YOU enjoy and things that allow you to be just you ... away from the kids and the spouse ... you will be so much better for others. Not only will it allow you to enjoy life just a bit more, but it will also allow you to be more present for others. I mentioned this earlier in the book: you are of NO good to anyone if you can't first learn to take care of yourself. No matter how pretty the smile you manage to put on your perky little face, no matter how much fun you *claim* to be having in your life, you will be nowhere near fulfilled if you don't allow yourself time to spend with friends, just being girls! When you were a teenager and had extra time in your day, what did you do? Did you run home and fix dinner for your parents? Did you take your free time in the evening or on weekends to work on an extra homework project or to make sure your room looked just perfect—without a speck of dust or a thing out of place? Heck, no! You were begging your parents to let you go out and play!

Somewhere between childhood and adulthood, we lost this. We lost the ability to just have fun. Especially as women, and doubly as high-strung executive types, we have completely forgotten how to slow down and to just be us! Somewhere on the journey between childhood and adulthood, it was ingrained in us that every spare second we have needs to be used for the betterment of someone or something. And if we weren't doing this, we were in some way failing! This is huge self-defeating behavior. We all need time to work on the betterment of ourselves, which includes allowing for a little "me time." I am not advocating that we all need to run out in the evenings, grab our girlfriends, and play a quick game of red rover (although it'd probably be pretty fun—I've packed on a few pounds since third grade, so I feel confident that I could break right through that human chain!). What I am doing is giving you permission to take time for yourself. In fact, I am insisting on it.

My guess is that you will be all over this one. You're going to run right out (if you haven't already) and wrangle up a few friends for your first big outing in a really long time. And I also guess that you're gonna have a blast. But … *and this is a big but* … my guess is also that most of you will stop after that first outing. And if you do this, you will have accomplished nothing. You will have failed at making this a consistent part of your new better life. Again, I am not advocating that you need to be hitting the club scene every Friday night like some of the cougars I see out there. But there does need to be some consistency in it. You need to always make sure you are taking time for just you. And you will be a better gauge of when you are in need of this than anyone. *When* (and I say "when" instead of "if" because I know it will happen … it does to each of us) … *when* you feel like you are about to "lose it" and are at the end of your rope, you HAVE TO take some "me time."

You may need to refer back to this chapter from time to time, and that's OK. Remember: the stronger and more refreshed you are (hangover from girls' night excluded), the better you are for everyone else. Good luck. And for the love of Pete … have some fun!

CHECKLIST

○ Develop a plan for your "alone time"

○ List the girls you want to invite out for girls' night

○ Plan (and execute) your first girls' night out

○ Research some social organizations in your area

○ Attend an event with one of these organizations

○ HAVE SOME FUN!

Chapter 14

YOUR JOURNEY HAS JUST BEGUN

"Life isn't about finding yourself. Life is about creating yourself."

—GEORGE BERNARD SHAW

WELL, GIRLS, WE DID IT! We've traveled quite a long way on our journey, and now it's time for the rubber to REALLY meet the road. While our trip together is coming to an end (for now), as individuals you have just started on the journey toward the rest of your life.

Let's take some time to reflect on what you have learned on our ride:

· ·

- You have outlined your values, strengths, and passions.
- You have decided whether you're working in the right profession or with the right company—and if you're not, you're on your way to making some changes.
- You mapped out your ideal day—how you'd like to spend your time and whom and what that time is focused on.
- You have made sure that the people you surround yourself with are building you up ... and not tearing you down.

(continued)

· ·

- You have gotten your spouse on board (OK, OK ... for some of you I know this one might take a little while, so suffice it to say that you've at least got 'em on the right track!)
- You have taken a close look at the things holding you back and have mapped out a plan to address them.
- You have worked to create a powerful presence and are actively working to claim that power.
- You are *actively* working to "not sweat the small stuff" and have your accountability partner keeping you in check.
- You are consciously infusing laughter and connection into each and every day.

And finally ...

- After all this hard work, you are making absolutely certain that you are carving out time for Y-O-U. Remember, moms: you will be absolutely NO good for anyone else if you don't take time to build, cherish, treat, grow, and challenge YOURSELF!

WHEW! We have done a ton of work. I'm tired just reading over the list. But this work is imperative if we want to lead fulfilled lives. And isn't that what we are all really after? The chance to lead a rich and rewarding life. And to do this all while taking care of ourselves and our families. It IS possible to create the life you've imagined. It IS possible to be the wife, the mother, the daughter, the sister, and the friend you know you can be. It just takes work—the work we've already outlined here.

Let's reflect a bit more. Take a few minutes to write out your top five take-aways from this journey. And then take it a step further. Describe what changes you have *already* made, and what you plan to *continue* doing to move further toward making that item a permanent fixture in your life:

Take-away	What I DID and what I will CONTINUE doing

First, heartfelt kudos for the items above that you've already begun to tackle. But mama didn't raise no fool. I know there is plenty more to do ... and I'd be willing to guess, at least one or two of the items you listed above are easy ones (look above ... how many of you listed having a regular girls' night out as one of your items?). Don't get me wrong—it is a fabulous item (and I'd definitely list it on my top five too), but you need to ensure that you include some of the more challenging items on the list. I know beyond a shadow of a doubt there are items mentioned in this book that you completely skipped over—either because you felt there weren't important or, more likely, because they were scary to even think about addressing (like telling that energy-sucking naysayer of a friend of yours to shape up or ship out!). My guess is that those items ... the tough ones ... aren't the ones you listed above! Am I right?

Well, I'm not going to let you off the hook that easy. It's like your kids do when you ask them to clean their room—they sweep all the stuff they don't want to clean up under the bed … out of plain view … just hoping you don't find it! Well, I am NOT falling for that trick. I'm a mom and I know to look under the bed … and I am going to make you pick up every last item … including the ones you don't want to! Only then will you have reached your destination—that of a clean and fulfilled life! Back in Chapter 1 you signed a pledge … a pledge that stated you would be all in … that you would work through ALL the exercises and would allow yourself to try new things and to forgive yourself and get back on the horse when you made some mistakes along the way!

So where did you slack off? Thumb back through the pages of our journey to see which exercises you may have left blank (if we're being honest, these were probably the items that scared the heck out of you!). Note the areas you still need to muster up some courage and work on. Ask yourself the following questions and check off each of the areas that STILL NEED SOME WORK:

....

- ○ Do I have a clearly defined set of values, which I stick to in ALL situations?
- ○ Have I taken time to identify my strengths and to make sure I am putting them to good use in both my personal and professional life?
- ○ Have I uncovered what I am really passionate about … what I *really* want to be doing with my life?
- ○ Am I in the right career? With the right company? (And if not, what am I doing about it?)
- ○ Do I have a clearly defined "ideal schedule" and does it incorporate each of the seven areas we discussed: self, spouse, children, family, career, friends, and community?
- ○ Am I surrounding myself with the right people? (And did I get rid of the ones who aren't?)
- ○ Is my spouse on board and supportive? And does he/she carry his/her share of the load?
- ○ Do I have a plan to tackle all the THINGS holding me back?

....

○ Do I have a powerful presence and am I claiming that power?

○ Have I learned to "not sweat the small stuff" or am I still freaking out over the non-important?

○ Do I find something to laugh about (I mean a really belly laugh) and someone to really connect with each and every day?

○ Have I found a way to squeeze a little "me time" into this crazy-hectic life of mine?

....

Talk about these with people (your accountability partner, your spouse, your girlfriends). Let them know that these things are a struggle for you. I'd be willing to bet you receive support from people and places you never imagined. Come up with your own **Checklist** of things left to do to further you on your journey. And refer back to it often! It takes time to build a habit ... and I promise you, the time you spend building the habits outlined in this book will pay off in more ways than you can imagine.

But let's keep it real. Even with creating and living the life you've imagined, you will still get tired, you will still have days when you just want to lose it, and you'll still have days that you go to work with a huge smudge of kid goo on your shirt! We ALL do. These are the days to rely on your girlfriends to pull you up. Talk to the other working moms in your network—because, trust me, we all have those days! But isn't that what makes the journey interesting!

I have no doubt that each of us can create the life we want to lead, and live it with passion and purpose. We just need to fix what needs fixing (as we have addressed here), keep moving forward, and for goodness' sake ... cut ourselves some slack! Life is about being the best, most powerful and passionate YOU possible ... and loving the journey! It is not about being perfect, it is not about catering to other people's every whim, and it is definitely not about balance. If you think about it, there is really no such thing as *balance*. I mean really, you've seen our schedules and our to-do lists—the scales tip almost hourly! Yet, as working moms, I believe we CAN still have it all ... just not all at once! :)

As we end our girlfriend road trip and as you continue working on the items outlined on our journey, remember two important lessons:

Love Life ... Love What You Do ... and Have Fun!

AND

D.S.T.S.S.A.R.I.A.S.S.

Kristin Andree's mission is to *"coach, challenge, and empower others to lead passion-filled, powerful, and prosperous lives."* After years of climbing both corporate and entrepreneurial ladders of success, Kristin decided that there was more out there for her ... that she was not yet leading the life she desired. With some soul-searching, a good hard look at her life (and the people in it), and a dose of hard work, Kristin was able to create the life she'd always imagined. And the path to leading such a fulfilled life is what she has captured in these pages.

Kristin is a speaker, an author, and president of Andree Media & Consulting, a coaching and consulting firm that teaches clients exactly how to reach the pinnacles of success in business and in life.

Kristin resides in Southport, Connecticut. And, when this busy mom manages to sneak in some free time, she enjoys fashion (especially the accessories), traveling (tropical locations are her favorite), music (good 'ole rock and roll) & theatre (being close to NYC does have its advantages). Above all, treasures spending time with her husband & their three daughters: Bailey, Mia and Kennedy.

www.andreemedia.com

Recommended Reading

Here are a handful of books I think are just fabulous...

Now Discover Your Strengths
by Marcus Buckingham and Donald O. Clifton

And the updated version...
Strengthsfinder 2.0
by Tom Rath

Anything from the *Don't Sweat the Small Stuff* series
by Richard Carlson, Ph.D.

The Energy Bus
by Jon Gordon

Never Eat Alone
by Keith Ferrazzi

Who's Got Your Back
by Keith Ferrazzi

If You Don't Have Big Breasts, Put Ribbons on Your Pigtails
by Barbara Corcoan

····· 100 Things to Do Before I Die ·····

1
2
3
4
5
6
7
8
9
10
11
12
13
14
15
16
17
18
19
20
21
22
23
24
25
26
27
28
29
30
31

32 ....

33 ....

34 ....

35 ....

36 ....

37 ....

38 ....

39 ....

40 ....

41 ....

42 ....

43 ....

44 ....

45 ....

46 ....

47 ....

48 ....

49 ....

50 ....

51 ....

52 ....

53 ....

54 ....

55 ....

56 ....

57 ....

58 ....

59 ....

60 ....

61 ....

62 ....

63 ....

64 ....

65 ....

66 ....

67 _____
68 _____
69 _____
70 _____
71 _____
72 _____
73 _____
74 _____
75 _____
76 _____
77 _____
78 _____
79 _____
80 _____
81 _____
82 _____
83 _____
84 _____
85 _____
86 _____
87 _____
88 _____
89 _____
90 _____
91 _____
92 _____
93 _____
94 _____
95 _____
96 _____
97 _____
98 _____
99 _____
100 _____

Household Responsibility Chart

Mom	Dad	Kids	Hired Help	Shortcuts